How PARLIAMENT works

How PARLIAMENT works

JAMES MARGACH

Political Correspondent of
The Sunday Times

Tom Stacey

First published in 1972
by Tom Stacey Ltd., 28-29 Maiden Lane London WC2E 7JP

ISBN 0 85468 033

Printed in Great Britain

by The Garden City Press Limited, Letchworth, Hertfordshire SG6 1JS

CONTENTS

AUTHOR'S NOTE

Parliament has been brought closer to the public than ever before by modern mass communication. This book is designed to answer the many questions posed by this fact, and to satisfy the lively and intelligent public demand for more information and background about the modern structure and exercise of power, covering Parliament, Government, Cabinet, Whitehall and the Political Parties, explained in non-technical terms.
It explores the systems of government in a way that will appeal not only to the general reader with an alert interest in what goes on at Westminster, but also the student who needs a commentary shorter than Bagehot yet more elaborate than a guidebook.

JDM

PHOTOGRAPHS and documents have been kindly lent for publication by the Central Office of Information and The Sunday Times.

CHAPTER I

How it all began

In order to understand Parliament today it is essential to know some of Parliament's history over the past thousand years and to take a short backward glance at the main events which have combined to fashion the present institution. That our system of Parliamentary democracy is unique in the modern world is no idle boast. Should you visit Westminster and feel perhaps slightly bewildered by some of the archaic procedures and rules you see and hear in both Houses, remember that it is a thousand years of history in action and that the centuries of the Saxons, Normans, Tudors, Stuarts, Hanoverians and others have each added their contribution to the present-day fabric of Parliamentary government.

The British Parliamentary system of today has inspired the spread of democratic Parliamentary government to the whole world and is a wonderful example of how ancient and modern may be merged into an instrument of authority tempered with freedom.

Because we invented it some eleven to twelve centuries ago, we have had more experience in making the system work than any other country. When one sees new countries having difficulties trying to graft the Westminster model on to their Asian, African, Caribbean or other native cultures, it is unrealistic to be impatient.

The present-day British Parliament is the distillation of

various cultures, native and imported. Many people think that constitutional history only started with William and the Normans in 1066, but the surprising thing is that the first experiments in creating the theory of Parliament and Government as we know it today were taken long before Hastings. So we must honour the Saxons as the real pioneers and founding fathers. Their system may be traced back to Ethelbert in the sixth century. Among the Saxon kings who followed him were Alfred the Great, Edward the Elder, Edgar, Egbert (who created a 'united kingdom' of England in 829), Ethelred, Canute and Edward the Confessor – they provide the roll-call of early rulers who first adapted Saxon tribal habit to governing the country with the agreement and consent of the governed. They called their system the *Witanagemot* – the old name for an assembly.

The Witan system was élitist, representing the exclusive establishment of the time; in the modern sense they were organized as caucuses. Each king took counsel with the leaders from the regions and shires. Although the crown's patronage was supreme, the successive Witans were not rubber-stamp assemblies. They wielded enormous power, equal in some respects to those of popularly elected Parliaments of twelve centuries later. They could elect kings, and then overthrow them; they legislated after debating the issues involved. At the same time the outlines of latterday local government also started to take shape under the Saxons; the members of the Witans were accepted as the local leaders, thereby providing the earliest known links between the King's Court and Council and the people. The current prominence given to new theories of regional government and development is not all that novel; the Saxons were eleven centuries ahead of us!

One representative Witan may be cited: in 934 it met at

Winchester, the old capital city, attended by 2 Archbishops, 4 Welsh kings, 17 Bishops, 4 Abbots, 12 Ealdermen and 52 *ministri* (landholders). The point to note is that the Witan members were not popularly elected by voters, but were there because they represented the shires and other areas (the beginnings of the constituencies). The Saxons pioneered well; they understood early the wisdom in statecraft of combining the Crown, State, Church and People in a workable single system.

After the Saxons came William and the Normans, with new despotic ideas from the continent. But wisely they did not destroy the Saxons' Witan system. Indeed, William built upon his predecessors' foundations, transforming their Assembly into his Great Council, six times greater in number – the Conqueror's Councils comprised about the same strength as the House of Commons of today with 630 members.

The Normans, while strengthening their kingly grip on power at the centre through their Great Councils, proceeded to expand their rule into the countryside, by a rapid extension of the feudal system. This meant making gifts of land to the barons, who in turn accepted responsibility for their tenants and workers. This was the start of government by Kings and Barons in the earliest of coalitions.

Reforms and new freedom did not come in stately procession. Some rulers made significant advances, but all too often a weak king or a civil war lost the ground gained, and reforms had to be extracted painfully and at severe cost in cruelty and suppression.

Hence the historic importance in Parliamentary history of the Magna Carta, which was signed by King John at Runnymede in 1245, under the *diktat* of twenty-five rebellious nobles. They compelled him to sign the pledge to govern in future by Rule of Law. The Magna Carta was the first Charter of Human Rights – rights which humanity is still battling to preserve, 700 years later. The growth of personal freedom, the rights of human beings, the curbs and cross-checks on our rulers – these processes started that day at Runnymede. Historians in succeeding generations have saluted the occasion as the beginning of responsible and representative Government, because Magna Carta led by stages to the expansion of the direct representation of local leaders (though not to popular or universal suffrage until the wider reforms in the nineteenth and twentieth centuries).

Other major landmarks followed. Simon de Montfort summoned a famous Parliament on 20 January 1265, famous because this is the earliest surviving list of those issued with the Writ of Summons. The term *Parliamentum* had been in use already for thirty years. Then in 1295 Edward I summoned what has since become known as the Model Parliament—now accepted as the direct ancestor of our modern Parliament. The following decade saw a wider spread of representative bodies and institutions.

Edward's Model Members debated broadly the same topics as today's Parliament: chiefly the administration of justice, the rule of law, taxes, land and property. Indeed, the financial controls and procedures for grants and State expenditure still known as 'Supply' were initiated around 1400 in much the same form.

At about the same time, 1400, the independence of the House of Commons from the King was first asserted and displayed. Following the earliest selection of citizens, knights and burghers to attend Parliament as Members, it became the custom of the Commons to withdraw immediately after the State opening of Parliament to a separate meeting place of their own in the Chapter House of Westminster Abbey, to conduct their debates in freedom and independence. In 1547 they were given St. Stephen's Chapel in the Palace of Westminster (the entrance to the House of Commons of today) by Edward VI; and it continued as their meeting place until the fire of 1834 destroyed most of the Palace.

In earlier days Parliament was more mobile, frequently meeting outside London, with York as the most frequent alternative. The term 'House of Commons' first became established in the middle of the fifteenth century and the 'House of Lords' during Henry VIII's reign.

Throughout the centuries there were constant battles between Crown and Parliament, and the power struggle was always about the supremacy of Parliament to defend public interest and especially public funds from the constant demands of monarchs. Under wise sovereigns, notably Henry VIII and Elizabeth I – both of whom had the Tudor flair for surrounding themselves with sound advisers – Parliament's authority advanced with the growth of national prosperity, especially in the Elizabethan age.

All too often the power struggle was bitter and destructive. Sometimes the most important reforms were brought about by silent, bloodless revolutions. The Petition of Rights, accurately described as our second Charter of Liberty, after Magna Carta, became law in 1628, with the agreement of Charles I. This provided that no taxation could be imposed without the consent of Parliament. Even so, this did not prevent Charles breaking into the House of Commons in 1642, with soldiers, and ordering Mr. Speaker Lenthall to point out to him the five Members whom he suspected as being responsible for organizing the opposition to his demands.

Every schoolboy knows of the historic scene which

followed: how Speaker Lenthall, kneeling to show that no respect was withheld from the Crown, told the King that he, the Speaker, could neither see nor hear instructions from anyone other than the Commons themselves. Thus another great landmark in freedom was established and the independence of Parliament was asserted and accepted.

King Charles, alas, did not learn his lesson; his personal rule clashed with the Commons' ideas and interest and led to the Civil War (1642–1652), which ended in his defeat and subsequent execution on the gallows erected in Whitehall. Then followed another challenge to the growing but still weak Parliamentary system by Cromwell, who expelled the incumbent Parliament during the Commonwealth and tried a variety of hand-picked Parliaments as well as military and quasi-military assemblies. But the country's brief experience of Cromwell's form of dictatorship came to an end with his death in 1658, and it was the same Speaker Lenthall, who had defied Charles I, who led the rump of the Parliament outlawed by Cromwell back to power, carrying the mace, which continues to be the symbol of Mr. Speaker's authority.

There was yet another convulsion in the relations of King versus Parliament when James II, attempting to impose his Roman Catholic religion upon an unwilling people, asserted his father's notion of 'Divine Right' of kings and challenged the rule of Parliament by disregarding the Habeas Corpus Act of 1679 which protected citizens – and still does – from being sent to prison without public trial.

This challenge ended when William of Orange was invited to invade England, and James fled to France.

We now reach the third great landmark in the history

of our personal liberties. After a bloodless constitutional revolution the Bill of Rights of 1689 helped to establish the Rule of Law. This Act prohibited the King from passing illegal laws or suspending existing laws or imposing taxes, without the authority of Parliament.

These successive reforms combined to establish what is now known as 'the constitutional monarchy', which means in practice that the Crown's authority is vested in Parliament; in more formal constitutional terms, the Crown working through and with the House of Commons and House of Lords, in Parliament assembled.

It is worth noting that the Bill of Rights, which established the principle of constitutional monarchy which continues to the present day, led in turn to the development of the Cabinet system which is at the heart of our present-day structure of government. This system was really built upon the earlier Secret Cabinet (Cabal) system of Charles II's counsellors operating as functionaries of the Court. The development of Cabinet Government led in turn to the emergence of the Executive and Civil Service as the central instrument of government.

Most authorities are agreed that our two-party system dates from the same period. The then Tory party of country squires and rural interests started to come together behind King and Church, while the Whig landlords, aligning themselves with the commercial and trade classes, identified with Parliament.

The role of Prime Minister in the modern sense also dates from the same time. When the King was unable to preside over Cabinet meetings, the Prime Minister took over instead. From this grew the tradition of the Prime Minister being not only *primus inter pares* (first among equals) but also principal spokesman of the Government of the day in Parliament. (This is explained more fully in chapter 5: 'The Prime Minister'.) So the Witans of the Saxons, built on by the Normans, further developed by the Tudors, tested by the Stuarts, were finally given by the Hanoverians the features now easily recognizable at Westminster.

Like so much that is of the first importance in British history, Cabinet Government happened by accident, not by design. George I could not speak or write English, and George II was not very good at it. In any case, both were more interested in the affairs of their native Hanover than in setting up their new dynasty, and so naturally they left the running of the State to their Ministers and discontinued the practice of presiding over the Cabinet. Thus the Cabinet system developed to replace the monarch's function, and led almost at once to the emergence of the party system and party government. Formerly, Ministers acted for the Crown, individually and separately, without being organized as a group behind a united policy; they functioned as separate empires. Under the Georges, however, they started acting as a unified group and party under the Prime Minister, with Sir Robert Walpole recognized as the first of the line.

Since 1707, when Queen Anne refused to give the royal assent to a Bill passed by Parliament (The Scottish Militia Bill), no sovereign has refused to withhold constitutional assent to statutory legislation passed by both Houses of Parliament. By precedent – which is the British substitute for a written constitution – no monarch may now withhold assent from legislation passed by both Houses.

After the long, slow capture of power by Parliament, through the Cabinet system of Walpole, the Saxon machinery of rule by consent of the ruled became reality in the Reform Bill of 1832 and the subsequent extension of the Franchise by Disraeli.

CHAPTER 2

Three-in-one, Crown, Lords and Commons

Some people think that Parliament is the House of Commons and nothing else, perhaps because their sense of involvement comes only from their part in electing MPs at General Elections. Parliament, in reality, is a carefully balanced three-in-one, with the Queen, House of Lords and House of Commons forming the constitutional trinity.

Here we run up against an apparent paradox. We have a highly efficient form of constitutional government and our rights and freedoms are guaranteed by the Rule of Law, yet we do not have a *written* constitution. In the United States a copy of the written constitution may be bought across the counter anywhere. It runs to a dozen or so small printed pages setting out the detailed rights of all citizens, as first drafted in 1787, with amendments added later. But even if you cannot buy a copy of the British constitution in any newsagent's shop the reality is that your rights, freedoms and privileges are just as safe, precious and secure: they are established and protected by the Habeas Corpus Acts, the Bill of Rights, the Act of Settlement and many other statutes embodied in our Rule of Law. Britain's unwritten constitution enjoys much greater flexibility than a rigid clause-by-clause recital of rights and privileges – though it should be noted that prominent legal authorities frequently give an airing to the case for a written British constitution in order to protect the citizen's rights and preserve his liberties from being weakened and undermined by an all-powerful state.

This partnership of Crown, Lords and Commons is acknowledged in the preamble to every Bill, which always starts: 'BE IT ENACTED by the Queen's most Excellent Majesty, by and with the advice and consent of the Lords Spiritual and Temporal, and Commons, in the present Parliament assembled, and by the authority of the same, as follows:'

THE QUEEN In the partnership between Crown, Lords and Commons, the Queen's role within the Parliamentary structure is largely formal in the legislative sense, and is limited by the authority of constitutional monarchy. The Queen acts on the advice and counsel of her Ministers, the legal procedure which lies at the heart of our constitutional system. Clearly a severe crisis for Crown, Parliament and the State would arise if the Sovereign were ever to defy the advice submitted by her Ministers, among whom the Prime Minister is the chief Counsellor. The question, happily, is hypothetical; the will of the Sovereign is subject to law as much as our own.

But to imagine for one moment that the powers of the Crown are fictional is to overlook the mystical factor and the influence, the historical majesty, enshrined in the Queen, as part of 'Authority Transcendant and Absolute' which she effects with and through Parliament.

The Queen personalizes the continuity and central loyalty of the British people, completely transcending the role of an elective Presidential system. The Crown is the symbol of the country; and she wears the Crown of Edward the Confessor.

She reigns, but does not rule; she opens Parliament with

full State ceremonial, in the presence of Lords and Commons; she dissolves Parliament, Ministers are appointed and approved by her; the armed forces are her forces; her judges administer justice. The entire democratic and parliamentary system is personalized and symbolized in the Queen, reflecting and safeguarding the national unity of the State. The Queen in fact is three people in one: the visible tangible symbol of the State, the national source of power called 'the Crown' which is vested in Parliament, and last but equally important, she has the right to advise, warn and be consulted by her ministers – the Prime Minister must tell her every week what he has done with her country.

By contrast, the American President is like a limited monarch; often in conflict with his Parliament and acting independent of and contrary to the votes of the Senate and Congress in Washington. In Britain the Queen is the powerful symbol of government; many of the most important decisions are approved and promulgated by her at meetings of her Privy Counil attended by her Ministers.

The comparisons between the British Monarchy and the American Presidency have been described by Quintin Hogg (later Lord Hailsham, Lord Chancellor) in this way: 'Britain has become a republic with a hereditary President clothed in the purple and prestige of majesty. America, whose constitution is an earlier offshoot of the English tradition, in form a republic, is in fact a limited monarchy with an elective kingship guarded and hedged about with the checks and balances of a modified form of the British Constitution.'

Ronald Butt claims that the Reform Act marked the clearest point of distinction between the phase of British politics in which the Crown's influence could largely determine both the membership of the House of Commons and the way many of its members voted, and the period of party-based nineteenth-century politics in which a free electorate, however limited, decided the composition of the House and Governments. With the end of the rotten boroughs and the creation of new, larger constituencies which could not be bought or sold, the role was formalized for the constitutional Monarchy, which had to accept Governments and Ministers appointed by a Parliament which it could no longer control.

This important readjustment in the power structure has, surprisingly, added to the Monarchy's influence and strength. While it is true that the constitutional changes have deprived the Queen of many of the Crown's old-style prerogatives and privileges – in the sense that she has less direct personal power – she has become the personalized symbol of national unity, high above party divisions and factional arguments. In short, the Queen has become head of the family, and combines the mystical appeal of sovereignty with practical and personal influence as the permanent centre and symbolic expression of nationhood, as well as the figurehead of the modern multi-racial Commonwealth.

Our Monarchy, the oldest political institution in Europe apart from the Papacy, has surrendered many of its former prerogatives and sovereign rights, yet continues to reign with great splendour, enjoying nation-wide affection and loyalty and embodying common citizenship. The Queen represents all the British people in unity and is above faction. The British system is monarchical, but because the Queen does not exercise arbitrary power personally, and is thus above political battle, the Crown becomes an even more influential symbol of continuity, unity and loyalty – concepts represented in most other countries by a flag. This British system is unique in the world, reflecting the national flair for commonsense and compromise.

THE HOUSE OF LORDS Next to the Monarchy itself, the House of Lords is the oldest part of the constitution – it is also the oldest and most influential second chamber in the world. The Saxon, Plantagenet and Norman kings, as we noted in Chapter 1, held their Great Councils, comprising barons, feudal landowners and princes of the Church – the last named accounts for today's use of the terms: 'Lords Spiritual and Temporal' and the presence of twenty-six Anglican Bishops in the House of Lords, headed by the two Archbishops.

The present membership of the House consists of:

Peers of the Royal Blood	4
Archbishops	2
Dukes	25
Marquesses	30
Earls and Countesses	163
Viscounts	109
Bishops	24
Barons and Baronesses	702
	1,059

These constitute the Upper House of Parliament, whose members are entitled broadly to the same powers and privileges as Members of the House of Commons (though the Commons, being the seat of real legislative power, is very much the dominant partner). Here one refers to the House of Lords in its Parliamentary, constitutional and legislative sense. There is, however, the House of Lords in the legal sense, and this consists of ten Law Lords, or

Lords of Appeal in Ordinary, who sit as the Supreme Court of Appeal, the highest legal authority, functioning under the Lord Chancellor, the supreme head of the judiciary. The Lord Chancellor has a dual role, occasionally contradictory. In addition to being the Lord High Chancellor of England, presiding at the apex of the legal system, he has a special political role as member of the Cabinet of the day. As head of the judiciary he is above politics; as a member of the Cabinet ranking next to the Prime Minister in seniority, he can make controversial speeches in the political cockpit, just like other Ministers. On Government policies and in all major debates he is usually the Government's principal spokesman in the Lords.

While the House of Lords has broadly the same legislative function and constitutional powers as the House of Commons – all Bills for instance, go through the same stages in both Houses, and neither House can legislate on its own – there are important differences. Because of the constitutional crisis created in 1909, when the Lords refused to pass Lloyd George's 'People's Budget' and the then Liberal Prime Minister, Mr. Asquith, threatened to swamp an overwhelmingly Conservative House by creating 500 new Liberal Peers, the Parliament Act of 1911, passed after the most bitter political strife, severely restricted the Lords' powers on financial matters. Today the House of Lords has no power to amend, delay or reject any financial provision proposed and passed in the Commons – thus acknowledging the supremacy of the Lower Chamber as the elected House in the field of money, taxation and supply. In the event of a deadlock between the two Houses, the Upper House has the power to delay the contentious legislation by a maximum of fifteen months. Such a constitutional crisis is very rare indeed, but the reserve delaying power has proved an important brake and safeguard against hasty legislation, and like any second opinion, the House of Lords is a valuable sounding board for the ideas promoted in the Commons.

In modern conditions the main functions of the Lords are

i) To revise and closely scrutinize Bills sent to them from the Commons – and in this revising, refining and improving task they are superb, because of the vast experience and knowledge concentrated in the Upper Chamber.
ii) To delay a contentious Bill long enough to give everyone, notably the Government and Commons, a chance to have second thoughts.
iii) To initiate non-controversial measures on their own and send this legislation to the Commons.

They are also able to debate major national or world issues more frequently and at a higher level than the Commons, who are normally hard-pressed and over-disciplined by legislation and the Whips; and they can turn their attention to other worthwhile subjects which are seldom debated in the lower house.

For very important debates, between 300 and 400 Peers may attend, but only on rare occasions on this scale; usually about a hundred are in regular daily attendance and these are mostly experienced Parliamentarians, many of them elevated from the Commons, and others with a long hereditary and personal tradition of public service. The spectre of 600 or 700 so-called 'backwoodsmen' suddenly descending on Westminster from their stately homes in distant shires to pull off a coup in the division lobbies in defiance of their leaders, makes exciting headline reading, but it never happens in modern conditions.

Because of the nominally available Conservative majority which results from the hereditary element in the holding of titles, and its erstwhile identity with great wealth and privilege, campaigns for the reform of the House of Lords have been frequent over the years. Even the preamble to the 1911 Act, mentioned earlier, stated the ultimate objective as 'to substitute for the House of Lords as it at present exists a Second Chamber constituted on a popular instead of a hereditary basis'.

The reforms proposed from time to time by the Conservative, Liberal and Labour parties have been numerous and varied, while all-party committees have frequently tried to remove partisan prejudices in the interest of all-party unity. But the House of Lords, showing an astonishing capacity for survival, has outlived all efforts radically to change its composition and powers. The reformers have passed on: the House of Lords remains.

Many of the most striking of the proposals for changing the structure and powers of the House of Lords have come from prominent Conservative Peers belonging to famous titled families. Ambitious plans were put forward some forty to fifty years ago by such famous figures as the Marquess of Salisbury and the Earl of Clarendon: their plans – independent of each other and separated by several years – proposed a reconstituted House of Lords, consisting of 150 Peers elected by all their Lordships, and another 150 nominated and selected from outside. These and similar reforms advanced a half-century ago were invariably blocked not by the so-called reactionary House of Lords, but by timid Governments and by an even more reluctant House of Commons.

The Labour Party was also pledged to abolish the House

of Lords on coming to power, but Labour Prime Ministers and Labour Governments since those early days have been unashamedly expert in using the honours system for personal patronage, and have shown little zest for changing the Second Chamber. Both parties have also used the Lords as a dumping ground for elderly, unpopular or more often incompetent ministers and backbenchers. The most recent all-party reforms suggested made very rapid progress in 1969, with powerful support from leading Peers in all parties, but the opportunity was again lost, due to causes most of which had little or nothing to do with the future of the House of Lords.

As a revising, improving, scrutinizing Chamber, more independent from the excesses of party disciplines and able to act as a national forum on all major issues, the Peers render distinguished service to the country; particularly in the technical matter of going over new legislation more carefully and with greater legal and professional skill than can be attempted by the Commons; the Lords have an outstanding record in improving our laws and removing anomalies.

The history of the House of Lords reflects the transfer of power throughout the centuries from monarchs to the barons, then from the barons to the new aristocracy; then later again from the aristocracy to the new middle classes of wealth and newly acquired property; and more recently, in our day, from the wealthy industrial middle class and landed gentry to the newer professional, technocratic, and managerial social classes which have become established as a new focus of political power since the Second World War.

The House of Lords has taken each stage of historical change in its stride, and with characteristic English flair has absorbed each new wave of intake and reform. Which explains why the House remains very much in its own original mould, a hardy perennial, proof of the saying that the more it changes the more it remains the same.

The old tests of nobility before you could be ennobled – country gentlemen with broad acres, aristocratic connections, great wealth, property, the exclusiveness of class and record of service in maintaining the grand Imperial tradition – have mostly gone, overtaken and displaced by the new social and professional changes in the structure of our society; and this transformation has been speeded by the life peerage system which has been highly successful in providing the injection of new blood. About 200 life peerages have so far been created since the system was introduced in 1958. This new nobility is just as jealous of the influence and powers of the House of Lords as are the hereditary peers of long lineage. Both streams combine to maintain the independence of the Upper House; not being 'division lobby fodder' like the Commons, they are impervious to party Whips, and are not fussy over party labels for the good reason that they do not have to worry over constituents or sudden political squalls. After a thousand years, dating from those early Barons, their Lordships, whether lifers or ennobled for centuries, have a mutual determination to stay in business both from a sense of duty and of ordinary survival. Not that the life of a lord attracts princely rewards: Peers do not get salaries or any 'perks'. Their total payment is represented by the daily allowance for attendance of £6.00 (raised from £4 14s 6d in 1970) to cover necessary overheads in attending the House.

HOUSE OF COMMONS The House of Commons is the senior partner. The changing structure of power over the centuries, with the Crown compelled to surrender power to the earlier and rebellious Barons at Runnymede (chapter 1) and who later in turn surrendered supremacy to the Commons, leaves them in the position once held by the King. Now there are genuine fears that the trend is swinging too far the other way, with the elective Commons surrendering and sacrificing too much power to the Government and Executive represented by the Cabinet and the Whitehall complex of Government. The power of the Executive has increased enormously, at the expense of a House weakened in quality by the parties' need to impose uniformity of voting in order to stay in office. The party Whips who operate this system are also ensuring that the Cabinet and Government as a whole hardly need to persuade the House but can dictate at will; to this end the party candidates for election are seldom chosen for their firmly held original opinions. This is clearly going to be the big constitutional issue of the future.

The House of Commons today is composed of 630 MPs who are elected by a total electorate of some 39 million voters. Everyone of eighteen years of age or more is entitled to vote, with very few exceptions, among them being peers of the realm, bankrupts and felons not admitted to the polling register.

While it is true that neither House can legislate on its own, even the most militant critics of the Lords stop short of proposing a unicameral or single chamber Parliament for Britain. The fact that the House of Commons controls the purse-strings, and all budgetary, taxation and financial affairs, gives it the effective power. The Commons are very much the dominant partner.

Even more important, the lower House is the source as well as the vehicle of political power, controlling the stability and survival of the Government of the day. It is the first principle of Government that the Prime Minister and his colleagues, to survive in office, must retain the majority and confidence of the Commons.

The true functions of the Commons, according to one of the foremost authorities, the late Sir Ivor Jennings, 'is to question and debate the policies of the Government'. Here you should note an important distinction: that it is not the function of Parliament to govern, for that is the Government's responsibility, but to keep the Prime Minister and his Government under constant scrutiny, questioning and criticism. The House of Commons, in short, is nothing if it is not the great forum, the grand inquest, the national assembly, acting fearlessly as the custodian, safeguarding the nation's interest and the individual's rights and freedom.

In theory, the House of Commons controls the destiny of the Government, compelling the Administration to resign (if need be) and make way for another under a new Prime Minister, or to dissolve Parliament and hold a General Election. In modern times, however, the balances and checks are more subtle and sophisticated because of the power of the party machines, and it is nearly inconceivable that the majority party would overthrow its own Prime Minister and destroy its own Government. Cabinets are usually well warned in advance of the dangers facing them over the unpopularity of their policies, as the result of the subtle intelligence system which operates within each party; and once alerted to the dangers ahead they are usually able to take action to avoid serious defeat and the risk of being compelled to hold a general election before they are ready.

Nevertheless, there is growing concern over the decreasing authority and prestige of Parliament and MPs, due, on the one hand, to the increasing power of the party machines which undermines and destroys the independence of Members, and, on the other, to the self-interest of Governments, treating the House as a rubber stamp, as the servant and no longer the master. The danger of this state of affairs is as serious as it is obvious.

It is probably extravagant to say that Governments of all parties nowadays pay more attention to what the opinion polls, television, etc. are saying than they do to what MPs and the House of Commons are saying, but there is substance in at least identifying the trend. Both Houses will get the opportunity to correct this and restore their authority when and if they agree to admit the television cameras to their proceedings.

MPs' salaries were increased from £3,250 to £4,500 early in 1972, plus free air and first-class rail travel between constituencies and Westminster, with new additional allowances for London accommodation; at the same time, the secretarial allowance was raised from £500 to £1,000; Members have also free phones, free postage, a car and travel allowance within constituencies; wives are given ten free journeys a year to Westminster.

The salary increases and the more generous allowances recognize the modern trends and pressures which make MPs full-time career politicians. Critics complain that these factors will in turn make MPs less independent-minded and more amenable to whipping disciplines. These fears are exaggerated; the Chief Whips of all parties are never short of rebels. It would be a misreading of the position at Westminster to imagine that independent MPs have no role because of Government pressures and the squeeze applied by the Whips to make them toe the line; it should be remembered that recent major social reforms in Parliament, dealing with divorce, hanging, homosexuality, abortion, the permanently disabled and many others, were successfully carried through all their stages on the initiative of private MPs promoting their own reforming Bills.

In day-to-day business, in theory and practice, the Government is responsible to the House of Commons, from whom it derives its support and confidence. The Commons have also in reserve the penal power to throw out not only the Prime Minister but his Government as well; defeat for the Prime Minister and Government on major policy, in theory at least, would precipitate a General Election. This, however, would require a serious split in the ranks of the Government party, as well as in the Cabinet, events which are very rare indeed.

It is many many years since the House of Commons by its vote overthrew a majority-based Government; indeed, it is more than a hundred years since the Gladstone Government was banished from power as a result of a split in the Prime Minister's party in 1866. Prime Ministers are more vulnerable than their Governments, as the result of pressures in the governing party to change the leader but not the Government. It was a hostile Commons vote in 1940, for instance, which compelled Neville Chamberlain to resign, and it was Westminster opinion which made Winston Churchill the natural and acceptable successor as Prime Minister (he became party leader later). The point to note is that the overthrow of one Prime Minister and the selection of his successor both derived directly from a Commons vote and the pressure of Parliamentary opinion. That, one should add, was in war-time, and led to the formation of a Coalition of all parties, which lasted for five years until the war ended in 1945.

In theory, an incumbent Prime Minister can try to control his rebellious MPs by threatening to dissolve

Parliament and demand a General Election. The idea is that by seeking a new mandate and vote of confidence from the country the Prime Minister would at the same time frighten the rebels in his own party by putting their seats in hazard. This idea of how power operates is seriously at fault; a Premier is the last person in the world to cut off his nose to spite a rebel's face. Some Prime Ministers have played this one occasionally, by threatening to appeal to the will of the people, though it is very doubtful whether they would ever sacrifice their Government and party in high-handed fashion just to get rid of a few rebels.

In practice, the power balances operate with much greater sophistication. Parliaments are elected for a maximum period of five years, which gives the Prime Minister room to manoeuvre (for he alone decides the timing of the election, usually some time after 3½ years or so in office). Minority Governments, on the other hand, have frequently collapsed after short runs; as Disraeli said: 'this country doesn't like Coalitions'.

The entire Parliamentary structure in our constitution is based on the two-party system, with the Conservative and Labour parties forming the alternating Governments and Oppositions, changing roles periodically according to the General Election results (with the Liberal party represented by a small group of MPs, as the minority party, whose presence serves to underline the country's preference for two-party rule).

This means, in turn, that in the Commons the Opposition has an official role in the working of the constitution, recognized by the salaries given to the Leader of the Opposition (£9,500) and to the Opposition Chief Whip (£7,500), paid to them not by their parties but by the State. This arrangement is peculiar only to the British Parliamentary tradition; the Westminster model of Parliamentary democracy has been exported to dozens of new independent countries in Africa, Asia and elsewhere, but the theory of Opposition has always been the most difficult to transplant, as proved by the many instances of one party taking over as the one-party authoritarian Government all too soon after independence, and declaring all Opposition parties and groups illegal, proscribing them as a threat to the security of the State.

In this country, the Opposition in the House of Commons is regarded and accepted as offering the alternative Government-in-Waiting, and the Opposition leader is recognized as the alternative Prime Minister. Even so, an Opposition acts as though its primary purpose in life is to oppose for the sake of opposing; mostly it sustains a vigilant role of criticism and scrutiny, where possible amending Government measures introduced in the form of Bills. Only in extreme cases does an Opposition decide on outright obstruction of highly contentious and partisan Government legislation (Oppositions do not exist to make life easier for Governments); and where there is obstruction, Governments can always have the last word, in the House of Commons by introducing the guillotine, which sets a rigid timetable for getting the controversial Bills through.

These circumstances are relatively rare in the life-span of even the most controversial of Governments, for the House of Commons has assimilated the widsom of the centuries by creating a subtle balance between the responsibility of a Government to govern and the duty of an Opposition to oppose responsibly. Clearly the whole Parliamentary system would be paralyzed if a Government were to become a dictatorship, riding roughshod over Opposition and private MPs, or if an Opposition's only aim was to make life impossible for the Government. The present Commons system operates with notable efficiency and fairness, due to the instinct acquired and perfected throughout the centuries for making Parliamentary democracy work.

The entire structure *could* collapse in chaos were it not for the intricate balances and counter-balances which make the system tick; even the procedures guarantee fairness and justice to all sides simply by superb and delicate mechanisms which, on the one hand, prevent a Government railroading measures through Parliament and, on the other, prevent an Opposition reducing Parliament to impotence and ridicule by exploiting the opportunities for obstruction.

As Lord Campion, one of the greatest authorities on Parliament, wrote retrospectively after a lifetime spent in its service as Clerk of the Commons: 'The wisdom of the whole House far exceeds that of any of its members.'

CHAPTER 3

A tour of Westminster

Both the House of Lords and House of Commons are within the Royal Palace of Westminster, which used to be the main residence of kings from the time of Edward the Confessor to Henry VIII, when it ceased to be occupied by the Royal Family, though continuing as a Royal Palace from 1532. The Palace today covers eight acres, including more than 1,100 rooms, over a hundred stairways and more than two miles of passages and corridors to explore, if you are feeling energetic. Three hundred statues stand on your route march, as well as more than a dozen bars, tea-rooms, dining rooms, scores of committee and interview rooms – even a barber's shop is included in the services provided for a self-contained community.

WESTMINSTER HALL A tour of Parliament should begin either through the St. Stephen's entrance opposite the Abbey, or through the gates leading to New Palace Yard, facing Big Ben and the Clock Tower. Big Ben, the most famous clock in the world, takes its name from Sir Benjamin Hall, who was First Commissioner of Works and the Minister responsible for its installation. Its accuracy is astonishing for such a giant; its minute hands are 14 ft long, which means a couple of hundredweights to be kept moving all the time, but the massive mechanism is never more than one-twentieth of a second out.

When Parliament is sitting, there is always a light shining from the top of the Tower. As the Speaker declared when he re-lit the lantern at the end of the war in April 1945 (it was extinguished during the war years, because it would otherwise have acted as a guiding light for enemy night bombers): 'I pray that, with God's blessing, this light will shine henceforth not only as an outward and visible sign that the Parliament of a free people is assembled in free debate but also that it may shine as a beacon of pure hope in a sadly torn and distracted world.' That is what Big Ben means to many people across the world.

The Clock Tower has its own prison cell to which MPs and members of the public who commit grave offences against the dignity and privileges of Parliament may be sent by command of the Speaker, acting with the authority of the Commons. But do not worry that you may be lightly despatched to the prisoner's room 320 ft above ground; true, it is kept in habitable condition, but the last occasion it was occupied by someone under sentence was in 1880, when Charles Bradlaugh, an MP, was sent there for persistently refusing to take the oath because of his convictions as a freethinker. His stand, by the way, led to the reform in the procedure, allowing MPs when they take their seat at Westminster the option of affirming instead of swearing on the Bible.

The best view of Big Ben and the Clock Tower is through the gates of New Palace Yard. *New* Palace Yard was first used by Rufus more than nine centuries ago, to distinguish it and Westminster Hall from the Confessor's Old Palace close by. Today, New Palace Yard, a lung of Westminster, is usually crowded with MPs' cars, though at one corner you will come across the mounting stones used by Members well into the present century to help them mount their horses.

Westminster Hall has more history within its walls than any other comparable building in the world. Parts of today's structure include sections of the original Hall, built in the period 1097 to 1099 by William Rufus. The present majestic Hall, 240 ft long, 70 ft broad, 92 ft high was built by Richard II in 1394 to 1399. His coat of arms, representing a chained hart, is repeated frequently along the string course. The sky can be seen through openings in the roof; these served the practical purpose of allowing the smoke from the medieval feasts and roasting fires to escape.

One wonders how such a towering and beautiful roof, with its spectacular carvings completed six and seven centuries ago, was ever erected, let alone how it has remained secure for these many centuries, without columns, pillars or any other visible means of support. It is known architecturally as a 'hammer beam roof', and has been described as without a rival in any part of the world, not only for the ingenuity of its construction but on account of the perfection and delicacy of its detail. When part of the roof had to be repaired some fifty years ago, because of the spread of the death watch beetle, the new oak beams came from the same Sussex forest that supplied the timber when the Hall was first built 600 years ago.

Westminster Hall has been the scene of all the great historic occasions of regal splendour and Parliamentary ceremonial, like Coronation feasts, State banquets, the start of the Law Courts. Simon de Montfort held his celebrated Parliament in 1265 here; all the famous impeachment trials from William Wallace, the Scottish patriot, in 1305, to the long running show trial of Warren Hastings, which lasted seven years ending in 1795; and the trials of Sir Thomas More, Guy Fawkes and Charles I took place under this roof. In more recent times the Hall has been the scene of joint assemblies of Lords and Commons to honour distinguished world leaders, and of the lying-in-state of Kings and Queens, as well as of national leaders like Sir Winston Churchill.

Up the wide steps at the south end, turn left into St. Stephen's Hall, the scene of many famous Parliamentary occasions as well as business sessions. Here, when Parliament is sitting, visitors wait their turn to pass into the public galleries to hear the debates. St. Stephen's Hall is the site of the old House of Commons chamber under many dynasties – the Tudors, Stuarts, the early Georges. It has seen momentous history, notably the invasions by Charles I and Cromwell and the murder, in 1812, of Spencer Perceval – the only British Prime Minister to be assassinated.

At the far end through the swing doors is the Central Lobby, which many identify as the centre of democracy, because during much of a sitting day it is humming with activity, like a main-line railway station or an international airport. This is where the visitors see their Members of Parliament about personal, family, business or other problems. Increasingly, in these modern times, MPs perform the functions of welfare officers and personal advisers in order to help their constituents solve their worries. It is in this Central Lobby, too, that representatives of pressure and other lobbies get to work by pressing their campaign representations on Members.

It is in the Central Lobby also that an interview can be claimed by filling in a green card addressed to your Member, stating name, address and the subject of discussion. This card will reach him within ten minutes if he is at the House. While waiting, you should look round at the Venetian mosaics, the elaborately carved bosses, the gloriously stained windows and the lovely panels of the four Patron Saints: St. George, St. David, St. Andrew and St. Patrick.

The Central Lobby links the two Houses of Parliament – the Lords to the south, the Commons to the north. Theoretically, from the centre of the Lobby the Speaker can be seen presiding over the Commons 70 yds away on one side, and, on the other, the Lord Chancellor on the Woolsack in the Lords, also 70 yds away, in the same line.

Taking the House of Lords first, there will be no difficulty in distinguishing between the two parliamentary halves of the Royal Palace if you remember that the Lords' is furnished in rich crimson leather and the Commons in drabber green.

THE HOUSE OF LORDS Linking the Central Lobby and the House of Lords is the Peers' Corridor, where hang eight paintings of the Stuart era, notably the embarkation of the Pilgrim Fathers from Southampton in 1620; Speaker Lenthall defying Charles I by asserting the privileges of the House of Commons when the king demanded that the five members should be identified; Lord Russell leaving his wife when going to his execution for complicity in the Rye House Plot; the expulsion of the Fellows of Oxford Colleges for refusing to sign the Covenant to extirpate Popery in 1648; and the burial of Charles I at Windsor.

One important feature common to Lords and Commons is that both chambers are identical in their rectangular shapes and lay-out. This is deliberate, because it acknowledges that Britain operates under an established two-party system, unlike the semi-circular layout in so many other assemblies of the world to accommodate the great number and variety of parties and splinter groups. (At one time in France, there were about thirty.) In this country there is a third party, the Liberals, with the more recent emergence of the Nationalist parties from Scotland and Wales; but their presence does not reduce the overall effectiveness and working of the two-party system.

The two chambers of Lords and Commons are thus made to measure for the two parties represented by clear-cut divisions between Government and Opposition, with no nonsense about a variety of competing groups in between. The secret of our constitutional system's smooth and efficient working is that the Government must expect to be in Opposition one day; while the Opposition regard themselves, and are so regarded outside, as the alternative Government-in-waiting. This helps to explain why this country has been providentially free from dictatorships (except for one brief period under Cromwell) and civil and political upheavals.

The Lords' Chamber is 80 ft by 45 ft and 45 ft high, with a gilt throne at the far end of the chamber, under a sober cover, but beneath that cover, splendid and glittering in gold and scarlet decorations, with brilliant gold leaf and emblazoned with the royal arms. The only time the throne is occupied is when the Queen attends for the ceremonial state opening of Parliament, in the presence of both Lords and Commons. She attends in her full regalia of crown and robes. On this occasion another chair, a couple of inches lower in height to signify the consort's relative position in the constitution, is placed for Prince Philip; a third on the Queen's right, is for the Heir, the Prince of Wales, when he attends with the Queen. The Prince of Wales is now a Peer of the Realm in his own right, entitled to sit in the House, since he took his seat as the senior ranking Royal Peer early in 1970.

Just in front of the red-carpeted dais on which the throne is raised three steps higher than the surrounding chamber, sits a bewigged and robed figure. He is the Lord Chancellor, presiding over the daily sitting of the House. He has been described as the Lords' equivalent of the Speaker in the Commons, but there are important distinctions. As Lord Chancellor he represents the Cabinet and Government, and speaks with their authority on official policies (whereas the Speaker is independent of Government and Party and does not make speeches). He sits on the Woolsack – and it is a sack packed with wool supplied by Australian sheep farmers as a reminder of what was once our staple trade; it looks uncomfortable, without adequate back rests or supports for his arms. Notice the three important articles of regalia beside him: his three-cornered judicial hat, the mace and the State's great purse, signifying his high office.

A plain table is brought, and placed slightly forward of the Woolsack, on such occasions as require the Lord Chancellor to make an important speech to the House as a whole. Upon this table he places his documents and makes his notes.

In the Commons when a Member finishes his speech, a dozen or a score or more other MPs on both sides will jump to their feet, anxious to 'catch the Speaker's eye' and be called to speak. There is no such scramble in the House of Lords. The order of speakers is arranged by mutual consultation in advance, and the debates proceed in stately procession and in balance.

Another thing: the House of Lords, despite its potentially overwhelming hereditary influence, does not bother itself seriously with too many restrictive rules and old

OVER PAGE:

The Yeoman Usher of the Black Rod is the official responsible for maintaining order in the House of Lords.
Once the Queen has taken her seat on the Throne, Black Rod is sent to summon 'the faithful Commons'.

LEFT:

MPs await Black Rod's summons to the House of Lords to hear the Queen's Speech.
The doors of the Commons Chamber have been slammed in Black Rod's face. He must knock three times with his rod to secure admission.
When finally admitted, Black Rod utters the Queen's Command for the presence of the Commons in the other House.

Led by the Speaker and headed by the Prime Minister and Leader of the Opposition, the Commons make their way to the Lords' Chamber – under the stern eye of Sir Winston Churchill on his new statue in the Members' Lobby.

HER MAJESTY'S MOST GRACIOUS SPEECH TO BOTH HOUSES OF PARLIAMENT

DELIVERED ON

THURSDAY, 2nd JULY, 1970

LONDON

HER MAJESTY'S STATIONERY OFFICE

9d. [4p] net

procedural motions: there is no closure to end a debate, no guillotine to compress debates and prevent partisan obstruction, no closing hour. So what would happen if a Lord decided to filibuster? Technically, another Peer could move that 'the noble Lord be no longer heard'. But this procedural device for shutting up a bore who has been drooling on endlessly for hours, has seldom been invoked in recent years.

Another difference from the Commons to notice: in the Lower Chamber the MPs, on divisions being called, shout 'Aye' or 'No' – with the Speaker ruling that the 'Ayes' or the 'Noes' have it. Not so in their Lordships' House. There they divide between 'Contents' and 'Non-Contents'. Parliamentary questions are put to the Government in the Lords, but there is no Question Hour as in the Commons. Questions are limited to four at the beginning of business but far less strictly limited as to the time allowed for Supplementary Questions, arising from the substantive ministerial reply. You will also find the debates are not only often of a higher level, but at all times more decorous and less partisan. The party system of course, also prevails in the Lords, but whipping and other forms of party disciplines are much more relaxed and civilized; and as if to emphasize that tough party dog-fights do not make up their Lordships' life, there is a considerable group of cross-bench peers (not the ten law Lords only) who sit mainly on the neutral cross-benches between the Government and Opposition sides. Cross-bench peers are the last of the independents and are not to be confused with a third party.

In any case, the quorum is three, a civilized display of independence and disdain on those efforts by Whips and their three-line summonses requiring attendance. No one yet has succeeded in treating their Lordships as 'lobby fodder'!

The Lords' Chamber is the perfect setting for the pageantry and glittering State ceremonial of the Royal Opening of Parliament, which marks the start of each new Session in October or November. The Queen drives in State procession from Buckingham Palace to Westminster, with her State robes and Crown, accompanied by Prince Philip and sometimes by the Prince of Wales as well. She enters by the grand archway of Victoria Tower and the historic Norman Arch to the Robing Chamber, where the royal procession is formed, with the officers of the Court and Household in brilliant robes and uniforms, and proceeds to the House of Lords.

Once she has taken her seat on the throne, the Yeoman Usher of the Black Rod is sent to summon the 'faithful Commons' to attend her Majesty, the MPs having assembled in their own chamber to await the call; and as Black Rod approaches the Commons, the doors of the chamber are slammed ceremoniously in his face, and he has then to knock three times with his black rod of office to seek admission. This odd little touch of defiance also has great significance, dating back many centuries to the early times when the Commons had to meet behind locked doors in order to preserve their deliberations from all intruders and agents of the kings. When Black Rod is finally admitted, he utters the Queen's command for the presence of the Commons in the other House to attend her Majesty, and led by the Speaker and headed by the Prime Minister and Leader of the Opposition they proceed to the Upper Chamber.

The State Opening is a gorgeously colourful and thrilling spectacle. Peers wear their scarlet and ermine-fringed robes, peeresses are gowned and bejewelled, Bishops and Judges are in the full glory of their own robes. As the Queen approaches her throne, the lights, previously dimmed, suddenly brighten into full glory to reveal a spectacular blaze of colour and brilliance.

When Parliament is fully assembled, the Lord Chancellor, robed in black and gold, kneels and presents the Queen with the 'Gracious Speech' which she proceeds to read, opening with 'My Lords and Members of the House of Commons ...' The Queen's Speech is written by the Prime Minister and the Cabinet and its main purpose is to set out the legislative plans of the Government for the next twelve months. The State opening is a ceremonial of outstanding beauty; a symbolic occasion representing many centuries of history.

The Lords' Chamber at the end behind the Throne and Woolsack leads to the Prince's Chamber, which is really the ante-room for the main chamber. It is of great beauty and rich colour; indeed most of the Lords' rooms, halls and corridors have a glorious colour and atmosphere of history and decoration unrivalled anywhere. The Prince's Chamber is built in the Tudor style, with a dozen bas reliefs in bronze, depicting famous events like the Field of the Cloth of Gold, Sir Walter Raleigh spreading his cloak for Queen Elizabeth I, Sir Francis Drake being knighted and the escape of Mary Queen of Scots from Loch Leven Castle. There is also a rich display of Tudor portraits.

Leading off from the Prince's Chamber is the Royal Gallery, which most visitors regard as a majestic hall of impressive perspective and splendour 110 ft long, 45 ft wide and 45 ft high. Dominating the Gallery are two huge pictures, painted in the water glass style; one representing the meeting of Wellington and Blücher after Waterloo, and the other the death of Nelson, both completed over a century ago. There is also a wonderful display of portraits of Kings and Queens. This has been the setting for many of the great constitutional conferences and ceremonials, both national and international, in honour of world statesmen and rulers.

The Queen's Robing Room is one of the most beautiful of the smaller royal apartments. Here her Majesty prepares for the State opening of Parliament, donning her robes and Crown. There is a dais at one end of the room for the Chair of State beneath a canopy. When the Commons' Chamber was destroyed by fire-bombs in 1941, the Lords vacated theirs to provide an emergency home for the Commons, and moved to the Queen's Robing Room, which served as the House of Lords for ten years.

HOUSE OF COMMONS Moving to the Central Lobby along the Commons Corridor, one passes eight fresco pictures of some of the historic events of the Stuart period: such as Charles II escaping after the battle of Worcester disguised as the servant of Jane Lane; Montrose being led to execution; Parliament offering the Crown to William and Mary in the Banqueting Hall in Whitehall; and Argyll sleeping peacefully before his execution for his attempt to free Scotland from James II.

The Members' Lobby, the ante-room to the Commons chamber proper, is 45 ft square, and is the scene of the greatest activity as Members and Ministers rush to and from the Chamber, gossip with each other or meet the political (or lobby) correspondents. By far the most striking feature of the reconstructed part of the building is the archway over the main doorway leading to the holy of holies, the Commons' chamber – where the chief attendant, by the way, still has a snuff mull to stimulate Members as they pass into the Commons: Churchill always ceremoniously paused every day for his pinch during most of his half-century at Westminster.

The Arch is built of old, weathered stone, recovered from the bombed building and is already known as the Churchill Arch. On each side of the doorway are the statues of Britain's two great wartime Prime Ministers, in symbolically defiant postures: Winston Churchill and Lloyd George, jointly keeping watch over the scene which each in his turn dominated. The Churchill statue was erected only a short time ago.

Other famous political figures and national leaders commemorated in statues in the Members' Lobby are Balfour, Asquith and Joseph Chamberlain. Those omitted are as significant as those honoured in the sweep of history; no decision is ever reached to honour (or even, by silence, overlook) a former Prime Minister or national leader until ten years after his death, a wise precaution to allow the controversies to subside and thus enable the statesman to be judged in the cool perspective of history.

On entering the chamber, one is surprised how small and compact it is. This is not the massive assembly hall which many people expect as the setting for historic debates and famous sessions; indeed, it is so small and cosy as to be intimate. This is not an accident. When the old chamber was completely destroyed by bombs in 1941, during a German air raid, Sir Winston Churchill proposed that it should be rebuilt in its old form, size and dignity, even on the old foundations which were intact. The chamber, which was wrecked by incendiary bombs, was of the same size and style as the much earlier one destroyed in the fire in 1834, which then derived from the fourteenth century chapel of St. Stephen's. As one of the leading authorities on Parliamentary procedure, Dr. Eric Taylor, has recently remarked, when making the point that it would be difficult to see how our procedure could function if the shape of the chamber were altered: 'it took seven years to build a new chamber: it has taken six hundred years to evolve our procedure'. The setting, style, atmosphere and procedures of the House of Commons have remained largely unchanged throughout many centuries, being adapted only slowly to the pressure for modernization by each new generation.

Modernists complain that the opportunity was lost in the early nineteen-forties to reconstruct the Commons on a grand, modern scale, incorporating features which distinguish Parliaments and vast assembly halls in other world capitals. In particular, some regret that the chance was missed to build a semi-circular hall, with a raised rostrum and the usual electronic devices like microphones, amplifiers, cameras and bright lights.

A new Commons in the round was considered, but rejected decisively. Sir Winston Churchill and the Parliament of the time decided that the circular setting, while it may be ideal for European and other Parliaments, where there are dozens of groups and small parties forever moving and seeking new alignments, was inappropriate for Britain which has mostly been governed by a two-party system (with the exception of the period of the Irish Nationalists and when the Liberal party was in decline before the emerging Labour party). So the chamber is built solidly in rectangular style, divided into two equal halves facing each other, most convenient for the two major parties alternating between periods of Government and Opposition.

If any MP decides to change his party allegiance – such an event has been very rare in modern times – he has to signal a complete break with his past and 'cross the floor', whereas in the semi-circular chambers overseas, he would have to move only a few places symbolically Left or Right, where he would align himself with his new group or splinter faction. (The growth of the political parties and the roles of Government and Opposition are studied in chapters 7 and 9.)

This explains why Churchill and his colleagues decided on the more intimate chamber as the ideal setting for debates and not a rostrum-orientated assembly hall which would encourage a totally different style of debate.

The present chamber indeed is so compact and intimate that it cannot seat more than two-thirds of MPs on the benches on the floor of the House. Of the 630 MPs today, only 437 can be present on big occasions on the floor; nearly 200 others have to use the galleries for overflow seats.

This was how Sir Winston Churchill (supported by the Parliament of 1943) saw the re-building problem: 'We began by shaping our buildings. Afterwards our buildings shape us.' He went on: 'The semi-circular assembly which appeals to the political theorists enables every individual and every group to move round the centre, adopting various shades of pink according to the weather changes. I am a convinced supporter of the Party system in preference to the group system ... the essence of good House of Commons speaking is the conversational style, the facility for quick informal interruptions and inter-changes. Harangues from a rostrum would be a bad substitute ... the conversational style requires a fairly small space and there should be on great occasions a sense of crowd and urgency.' Churchill claimed that the semi-circular assembly hall 'which gives every member not only a seat to sit on, but a desk to write at, with a lid to bang, has proved fatal to Parliamentary Government.'

On entering the Chamber from the Members' Lobby

the first feature which strikes the visitor is the big canopied chair at the north (or Big Ben) end of the chamber. There sits Mr. Speaker in full-bottomed wig, robes and knee-breeches. He is the custodian of the rights, privileges and freedoms of the House of Commons. Mr. Speaker is elected to the Commons as an MP too, but when he moves to the chair he assumes an independent status above party politics, while remaining a member. When he is elected Mr. Speaker, usually at the start of a new Parliament after a general election, by custom it behoves him to make gestures of reluctance to accept the high office – his two sponsors have to drag him gently by the arms to overcome his resistance. This is a reminder of the old days when the office of Mr. Speaker was a highly dangerous occupation. Now he is paid a salary of £13,000, with an official residence in the building, a generous pension, and prospects of a Viscountcy or Barony in grateful recognition for a public service which can be exhausting in Parliaments when there are constant rows and crises. The first Speaker in the long line was Thomas Hungerford in 1377, and during the next 300 years Speakers acted primarily as intermediaries between Commons and Kings – as honest brokers – until they became identified as the custodians and spokesmen of the freedom and independence of MPs.

Immediately in front of the Speaker is the 'Table of the House,' occupied by the three Clerks of the House, wigged and gowned too, the great authorities and counsellors on procedure and rules. In front of them on the table are the great tomes of reference; and at its far end are the two despatch boxes, bound in brass filigree, opposite which the front bench Ministers and shadow Ministers from the Government and Opposition speak during the debates. At the far end of the table, farther from the Speaker but at the end nearer the public galleries, is the mace in glittering gilt, resting on two hooks, which is the symbol of the Queen's authority. The mace is carried at the head of the Speaker's procession, which opens the daily sittings of Parliament at 2.30 pm, by the Serjeant-at-Arms. This Officer of the House is the Executive head of the administrative staff of the Commons under the Speaker. While the House is sitting he occupies a chair at the opposite end of the chamber from the Speaker, in court dress and armed with a sword.

In the event of grave disorders in the chamber, and if the Speaker 'names' a rebellious and defiant MP who refuses to withdraw from the House, the Serjeant-at-Arms has the Speaker's authority to compel his removal, be it necessary by calling up reserves from the corps of custodians and attendants under his command. These are known technically as 'badge messengers' – they wear what seems like evening dress with gold chains and badges to signify their duties – and mostly they are former Regimental Sergeant Majors or of similar Warrant Officer ranks from the services. It is most unusual for an MP to be physically removed from the chamber because of disobedience or resistance to the Speaker's commands. In extreme cases of uproar and indiscipline an MP could be sentenced to the clock tower by the Speaker, and kept locked up there in charge of the Serjeant-at-Arms.

In 1931, John McGovern, an Independent Labour MP, refused to leave the Chamber, when ordered to do so by the Speaker for causing disorder and defying the authority of the Chair, and had to be carried out by a team of custodians. About fifty years ago, John Beckett, a Labour MP, grabbed the mace during angry scenes in an explosive debate over the then scale of mass unemployment and made a dash for it, but did not get out of the chamber before being caught. Fortunately, MPs are better behaved and more amenable to authority and discipline than in former times.

Usually, when an MP is suspended for a serious breach of the rules – he is ordered to withdraw when the Speaker 'names' him for defying his ruling – he is not sent to the Tower as a prisoner, as in the old days, but is temporarily excluded.

Do not expect to see an MP suspended on your visit to the public galleries, because such disturbances are rare indeed. 'Naming' a member means exactly what it says. After disorders and defiance by the Member, Mr. Speaker rises and announces: 'I must name the Hon. Member for Such-and-Such, Mr. So-and-So, for disregarding the authority of the Chair.' Immediately the Leader of the House (a member of the Government) moves that Mr. So-and-So be suspended from the service of the House – a motion which is passed without a vote. The MP should then leave the Chamber at once, but if he refuses to budge, the Serjeant-at-Arms goes up to him, taps him on the shoulder, and whispers advice to withdraw. If the named MP continues to defy authority the Serjeant-at-Arms calls up reinforcements (doorkeepers and custodians) who use the minimum of physical force to carry him outside.

The suspension, for the first offender, lasts normally for five days, but if he has ambitions for repeat performances he is suspended for twenty days next time – and for the third and subsequent offences he is kept out until the House decides to allow him to return.

The Irish Nationalists were past masters in exploiting and defying the rules; thirty-seven of them were once suspended in one sitting day. But such excitements are only occasional nowadays.

If a visitor commits a disturbance by shouting or staging a demonstration, he is removed from the galleries by the attendants, and is confined in the Serjeant-at-Arms' room until the House rises. So be warned!

On the immediate right of the Speaker is the Government, or Ministerial, front bench, where the Prime Minister and members of his Cabinet sit, with five serried rows of benches behind them of Government supporters. On the Speaker's left is the Opposition front bench, with the party leader seated opposite his despatch box and directly opposite the Prime Minister.

Some of the quaint habits and procedures which sometimes mystify visitors have an importance and relevance stemming from history – and there is a lot of history and tradition at Westminster. For instance, when MPs enter or leave the chamber they bow formally towards the Speaker, as a mark of respect to him as the fount of authority. Some historians believe that this respectful gesture comes from the days when the early Commons met in the St. Stephen's Chapel and Members bowed to the altar to express their faith.

Then, during debates, when you are most anxious to discover the name of the MP speaking, you will be frustrated and puzzled by the astonishing anonymity of it all. You will never hear anyone in the chamber referred to as Tom Smith, Dick Jones or Harry Brown, for the simple reason that the rules of procedure do not allow MPs to be identified by their names.

For instance, if a Member wants to refer to another, say in his own party, he says 'My Honourable friend, the Member for such-and-such a constituency'; if he refers to a Member of an opposing party he drops the friendship bit and speaks of the 'Honourable gentleman, the Member for ...' naming his constituency. If the MP referred to happens also to have a military or other service title he is identified as 'the Honourable and gallant gentleman, the Member for ...'; if, again, he has a courtesy title as the son of a higher ranking peer, he is referred to as 'the noble lord'; and, finally, if the MP is a member of the Privy Council he is always referred to as 'the right Honourable gentleman, the Member for ...' Similarly, for women MPs it is a case of the 'honourable lady', etc.

The case for this courteous tradition of not naming names is that it discourages any temptation to be outrageously rude, and thus helps to preserve decorum and respect even in heated debates. The more accurate explanation, however, is that the habit of using constituency pseudonyms is a reminder to MPs that they are in the House of Commons not because they are Tom Smith, Dick Jones or Harry Brown, but because they are elected by popular democracy as the Member for Such-and-Such Constituencies – and it is the constituency which counts, not the name of the MP.

Then you will notice a red line in the green carpet, running exactly two feet in front of the front benches on each side of the chamber. In far-off days, MPs used to carry swords into the chamber, and the red line was their swordsman's line of demarcation, as it were; if they crossed the red line they might be able to injure their opponents on the other side, but the compulsion of the thin red line set a limit which made it impossible to reach the other fellow across the floor in a fit of angry belligerance.

Even today, when swords are no longer worn – a kilted Scot has to remove an offensive weapon like his dirk from his stocking in case of causing injury! – the red line helps to remind Members to put reason before passion. An obstreperous or over-excited MP might be tempted to go halfway, or more than halfway across the floor in order to challenge, scorn or even insult political opponents and shout ridicule at them. So the red line reminds such an MP to stay on his home ground; if he steps across it by an inch or two his critics will instantly shout 'Order! Order!' and he comes to heel. In any case, the rule is that MPs speak to and address the chair; when they forget this and start addressing another member as 'You' they are called to account, for only Mr. Speaker can be identified in this fashion; the other MP is always the third party.

Swords are not the only contraband around the royal palace these days. Briefcases, parcels, attache-cases, and umbrellas must not be carried into the chamber under any pretext; nor may MPs read newspapers while sitting on those sacred benches. The MP, all eager to unburden himself of his pent-up opinions, is entitled to use notes for his speech. But only to refresh his memory or to prompt him in the need to recall a crucial quotation or the carefully rehearsed witticism which he has momentarily forgotten. But no reading of speeches, please! If any Member tries to read from a manuscript, his critics will instantly point to the offence and the Speaker will call him to order. Ministers are allowed more latitude in using briefs and fully prepared speeches, because they are dealing with official policies which require explanation and detailed elaboration.

A division takes place physically. Unlike the deputies of other assemblies, MPs do not sit on their seats and record their votes by press-button mechanism. When the time comes for a vote to take place the Speaker rises and says (for example): 'The question is that the Bill be now read a second time. As many as are of that opinion say "Aye".' (Shouts of Aye in deafening chorus from the Government side), to the contrary 'No' (also lusty shouts of dissent from the Opposition benches). 'I think the

"Ayes" have it (defiant chorus of "No"). Clear the lobbies.'

The Government and Opposition MPs leave the Chamber, pressing through the lobbies which run parallel with the House itself, with the Aye lobby on the Speaker's right and the No lobby on his left. Both sides appoint two tellers each, one for each lobby. One teller counts and the other checks the voting MPs as they pass through the lobby check-points, while the Clerks of the House compile their voting lists. Then, when all the heads have been counted – a division takes between six and ten minutes – the tellers return to the Chamber and report to the Speaker:

The Ayes to the right...... 123
The Noes to the left...... 111

'So the Ayes have it,' announces the Speaker. And at once proceeds to call the next business.

On important divisions on major issues the results are often received with loud shouts of 'Hear – Hear, Hear – Hear'. This chorus is Parliament's traditional way of applause, because clapping hands, stamping feet and thumping desks are frowned upon; in moments of great elation or deep emotion MPs will jump to their feet and wave order papers and shout 'Hear – Hear, Hear – Hear' in honour of their hero, but without the ringing cheers usually heard elsewhere when people are moved deeply.

In the evening when the light is fading and MPs are finding difficulty in reading the Bills or Parliamentary documents in the gathering dusk, an MP does not ask for the lights to be switched on; instead, he asks Mr. Speaker 'May candles be brought in, Sir?' – which recalls the days when candles were the only source of illumination in the chamber.

The House is very touchy about any word which may be unparliamentary; if any Member calls another a liar there will be widespread protests at this reflection upon the honour of a fellow MP (all Members are accepted and described as 'Honourable Gentlemen') though the crisis is usually resolved by the Member withdrawing the offending phrase at the request of the Speaker.

There are some distinguished precedents showing how to get round the ban, headed by Winston Churchill's reference to another Member's statement as 'a terminological inexactitude'. Then there was the Irish Member who said: 'I may not call the honourable gentleman a liar, but I will say that if I saw him walking across Waterloo Bridge with Ananias on one side and Sapphira on the other, I should say he was keeping very suitable company.'

CHAPTER 4

Question Hour

On your visit to Parliament do not miss Question Hour which opens every sitting day. Go into the Central Lobby soon after 2 o'clock on Monday to Thursday when Parliament is in session (on Friday the House starts at 11 o'clock and adjourns at 4.30), because the House is usually overcrowded with visitors who have come either to seek out their MPs on personal or constituency problems, or to have a look at their representatives at work.

Punctually, a few seconds before 2.30 pm you will see the Speaker's procession approaching from his official residence under Big Ben, swinging silently along the corridor past the Members' libraries and smoking rooms and into the Central Lobby, where it will make a right-turn towards the Commons. It is led daily by a custodian, impressive in his chain of office, white bow tie, tail coat and breeches; he is followed by the Serjeant-at-Arms, in court dress, bearing the Mace, the symbol of authority; then Mr. Speaker in full-bottom wig and robe, and his train-bearer; then the Speaker's chaplain and counsel. As Big Ben strikes the first stroke of 2.30 pm, the Speaker takes his chair and the Chaplain offers prayers, which open every sitting.

If you are in the Central Lobby as the Speaker's procession approaches you will hear the Police Inspector –

ABOVE:
Clerks of the House of Commons seated at their table – number 4 in the plan of seating in the House of Commons.

OPPOSITE:
Key to the arrangement of seating in the House of Commons.

1 *The Speaker.*
2 *Prime Minister or Government spokesman.*
3 *Leader of the Opposition or Opposition spokesman.*
4 *Clerks at the Table.*
5 *Civil Servants in attendance.*
6 *The Table.*
7 *The Mace.*
8 *Government front bench, occupied by Ministers.*
9 *Opposition front bench.*
10 *Back benches.*
11 *Other opposition parties.*
12 *Serjeant-at-Arms.*
13 *Hansard and press gallery.*
14 *Members' side galleries.*
15 *Special galleries, including Peers', 'Distinguished Strangers', Diplomatic and Commonwealth galleries.*
16 *The Public gallery.*

OVERPAGE:
The Serjeant-at-Arms, bearing the Mace, the Staff of Office carried before the Speaker.

rrangement of Seating in the House of Commons

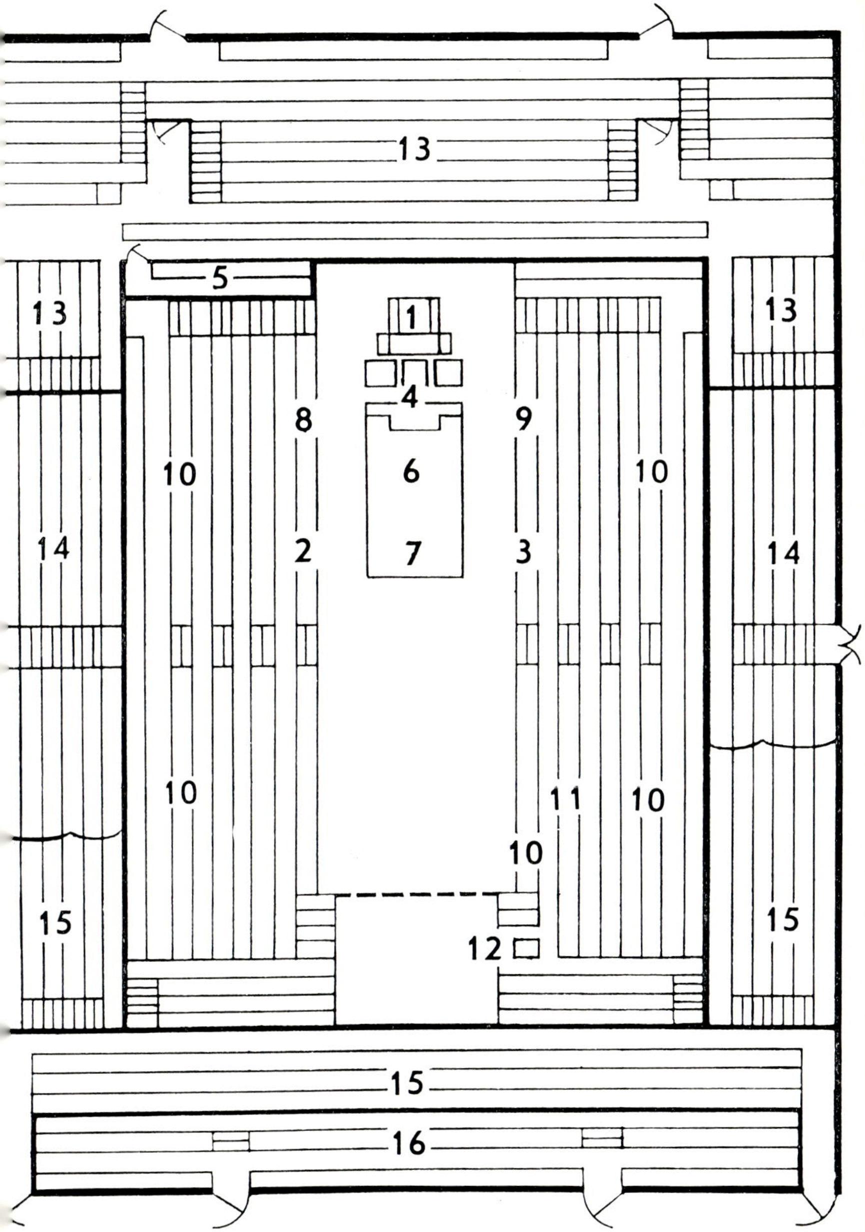

The Dispatch Box in front of the Prime Minister's seat, number 2 in the seating plan.

he heads the small police force at Westminster – call out the command 'Hats off, Strangers'.

Nearly forty years ago this coincided with a mass display of obeisance. Just as the Inspector called 'Hats off, Strangers,' James Maxton, the famous Independent Labour Party leader, who had a resounding voice which he knew how to use, rushed through the Lobby to catch up with another Clydesider, Labour MP Neil McLean. 'Neil, Neil', called Maxton, a split second after the Inspector had requested the visitors to remove their hats. So 'Neil, Neil' was regarded as the summons to 'Kneel, Kneel', and to the embarrassment and private merriment of the Speaker some five to six hundred people – it was the peak of the summer holiday season – knelt as though in prayer at the altar of democracy!

Immediately after prayers comes question hour, 2.30 to 3.30 pm which many visitors find the most fascinating part of the entire proceedings, because they see something which is not matched in all the assemblies of the world: a question hour when Ministers from the Prime Minister down to the most humble of departmental spokesmen in the Government are put under fire. For the next sixty minutes visitors can see powerful members of the Cabinet in succession going through a searching cross-examination from MPs of all parties. The nation's leaders are then treated almost as hostile witnesses. When the Prime Minister and Opposition leader and their respective teams are in top form the confrontation and exchanges provide as exciting a performance as any theatre.

Questions are numbered from one to a hundred and more, and grouped according to Ministers and Departments on a daily roster system, so that each takes his turn as first over the top. The Speaker goes through the list. He calls Mr. Smith, the MP who heads the question list

Opposite: The first page of questions notified in advance to Ministers. Aviation Supply was first on parade on this day, but the order varies from day to day, according to a roster system printed months in advance, so that MPs know when to time their questions. Note how the questions are answered on following pages from Hansard

today; the member rises and says 'Question Number One, Sir.' (It is easy to follow the questions and the identity of Ministers and MPs involved in the questions from the order paper handed out by one of the attendants at the door to the public galleries.) The Minister then rises from the front bench and reads off his prepared answer, drafted in most cases by his senior departmental officials who have usually a minimum of 10 days' advance warning when the Member submits the question to the Clerks of the Table.

Having given the substantive reply, containing the information requested in the substantive question, the Minister has to cope with a series of quickfire follow-up questions called 'supplementaries'. These are of course off the cuff, though here too the civil servants have done their best to anticipate the follow-up questions by drafting many background facts and figures to provide their Minister with handy ammunition in case of a running battle.

Ministers frequently establish Parliamentary reputations by their skill and ability in dealing with critical questions; and, most important of all, a Prime Minister cannot hope to dominate Parliament unless he establishes a powerful ascendancy during question hour. Two recent Prime

THE ORDER BOOK
OF THE
HOUSE OF COMMONS
from Wednesday 20th January 1971 inclusive

WEDNESDAY 20th JANUARY

Questions for Oral Answer

* 1 **Mr John Cronin** (Loughborough): To ask the Minister of Aviation Supply, if he will make a further statement on the progress of the Concorde supersonic airliner.

* 2 **Mr Neil Marten** (Banbury): To ask the Minister of Aviation Supply, if he will make a statement on future supersonic projects for the British aircraft industry.

* 3 **Mr Neil Marten** (Banbury): To ask the Minister of Aviation Supply, if he will make a statement on future sub-sonic projects for the British aircraft industry.

* 4 **Mr Ray Carter** (Birmingham, Northfield): To ask the Minister of Aviation Supply, what is the total of Government expenditure incurred since 1945 on civil aviation that failed to produce a commercial product.

* 5 **Mr Robert Sheldon** (Ashton-under-Lyne): To ask the Minister of Aviation Supply, if he will make a further statement on the Concorde.

* 6 **Mr Patrick Wall** (Haltemprice): To ask the Minister of Aviation Supply, if he will make a statement about the supply of heavy-lift helicopters to the Royal Air Force.

* 7 **Mr Patrick Wall** (Haltemprice): To ask the Minister of Aviation Supply, if he will make another statement on the progress of the Concorde programme.

* 8 **Mr Patrick Wall** (Haltemprice): To ask the Minister of Aviation Supply, if he will make a statement on the progress of the Anglo-French Jaguar Programme.

* 9 **Sir Anthony Meyer** (West Flint): To ask the Minister of Aviation Supply, what discussions he has had with European governments for the joint production and procurement of vertical/short take-off landing aircraft.

* 10 **Mr Cranley Onslow** (Woking): To ask the Minister of Aviation Supply, if he will now make a statement setting out the extent to which the Air Holdings orders for Lockheeds 1011s were underwritten by Her Majesty's Government.

* 11 **Mr John Wilkinson** (Bradford, West): To ask the Minister of Aviation Supply, whether he will now make a further statement on production funding for Concorde.

* 12 **Mr Robert Adley** (Bristol, North-East): To ask the Minister of Aviation Supply, whether Her Majesty's Government was a party to the contract between Rolls-Royce and Lockheed, under which Her Majesty's Government provided loan assistance to Rolls-Royce for the RB 2-11 contract.

* 13 **Mr Cranley Onslow** (Woking): To ask the Minister of Aviation Supply, if he will now make a statement on the recapitalisation of Short Brothers and Harland.

* 14 **Mr Patrick Wall** (Haltemprice): To ask the Minister of Aviation Supply, if he will make a statement on the provision of the new jet trainer for the Royal Air Force.

Ministers, Harold Macmillan and Harold Wilson, always tried to avoid outside engagements over lunch-time on Tuesdays and Thursdays – the days when 'Questions to the Prime Minister' are on the order paper – so that they could study their questions in detail, prepare their answers, and (the most crucial part of the preparation) anticipate the supplementary questions on which MPs would have become word perfect in the hope of causing the Premier the maximum embarrassment and ridicule.

Many backbenchers, too, have created reputations at Westminster by their persistence and skill in preparing their questions, an achievement in many instances of much painstaking homework on subjects which Members have made their own through specialization.

> Thus, if a Member rose to say
> (As Members do from day to day)
> 'Arising out of that reply...!'
> Lord Lundy would begin to cry.
>
> *Hilaire Belloc*

Even if the Lundys of this world on the Government front bench do not weep much nowadays, the author in his time has seen some Ministers brought near to nervous overstrain by a few awkward questions. Harold Macmillan, usually so imperturbable, was often in some state of nerves in advance of big Parliamentary occasions.

Each question is supposed to seek information and each reply is supposed to give the information requested, but resourceful MPs and Ministers being grilled very often develop a personal skill in scoring party political points – the ritual exchange of non-information.

Then the Speaker, having given the questions on the subject a fair wind (perhaps three or four supplementaries, according to the importance of the subject) moves on to the next question. 'Mr. Jones.' 'Question Number 2, Sir' – and off they go hammer-and-tongs.

Given a choice, you should try to be in the public galleries on Tuesdays and Thursdays. These are the days when the question sequence is interrupted at 3.15 for 'Questions to the Prime Minister'. This fifteen-minute session of questions is the great opportunity for the Prime Minister to make his impact; if he is to control the country he must first establish his command of the House of Commons; his speeches may be only infrequent at Westminster and in the country, but twice a week he has to go through the hoop in question hour when any failure to maintain his personal ascendancy weakens and undermines his stature as Premier and party leader. For those who like their politics life-size, the Prime Minister's twice-weekly performance is recommended as being a highly personalized battle with the Leader of the Opposition. Such a conflict is scarcely to be seen anywhere else in the world. In the United States, the Secretary of State and other Ministers are not members of the Washington 'Parliament', and thus have no critical Parliamentary Questions to experience every week – they have to use outside media and other occasions for getting across their departmental announcements and policies, hence the frequency and importance of press conferences. At Westminster all this is done under one roof.

Though our system of personal interrogation of Ministers is not as historic as many of the other procedures, the first recorded question was in the Lords in 1721 (their lordships are so often the pioneers and initiators) and the first printed list appeared in the Commons in 1835. On an average day there are over 130 questions on the list, though only about 35 to 45 are answered orally in the hour, and those which are not reached for answer publicly in the House receive written answers later.

At the close of question hour – 'Questions are the cocktails before the oratorical feast,' as Sir Ivor Jennings described them – there may be statements by one or more Ministers on particular policy announcements, on their own initiative, or often in answer to 'Private Notice Questions' on subjects of crisis or emergency importance, or of some pressing constituency question of unexpected importance; these 'PNQs,' as they are called, must have a substance and relevance approved by the Speaker in advance.

After that comes the main debate of the day, say a Second Reading of a major Bill, perhaps, or a defence or foreign affairs controversy, or a survey of the state of the economy. The sequence seldom varies. On Government business affecting the Government's overall responsibility, the Prime Minister or the senior Minister involved departmentally opens; on average he speaks for 40 to 45 minutes, sometimes longer, followed by the Opposition leader or a senior Shadow Minister from the Opposition front bench for another 40 minutes. From around five o'clock until close on nine the backbenchers have a free run, with the Speaker holding a fair balance not only between the parties but between the differing views within the parties. Then, shortly before nine o'clock, the front bench shadow Minister usually winds up for the Opposition, followed by a Senior Government spokesman (about 35 minutes each) and after that a division is called, with the 'Ayes' to the right and the 'Noes' to the left.

Following the conclusion of the main debate, there is always a half-hour adjournment debate which enables an MP – the subject and Member are selected and announced some days in advance by the Speaker – to initiate a debate on a specially pressing subject, usually of constituency importance; to which a Minister from the Department involved replies. These adjournment thirty-minute debates are invaluable, not only as a safety valve for controversial local topics but as a challenge to Ministers, as probing exercises demanding explanations of departmental action or negligence.

Many of these half-hour adjournment debates at the end of a long day frequently result from lively exchanges during question hour at the opening of the sitting. If a Minister, under pressure, has failed to give satisfaction by his answers, the aggrieved MP, very often on a constituency matter, jumps up and announces 'Mr. Speaker, Sir, I wish to give notice that owing to the unsatisfactory nature of the reply I propose to raise the matter on the adjournment.'

From 2.30 to 10.30 pm is the normal daily sitting. But what about all those night sittings you read about, with MPs, exhausted by overnight shift-work, having breakfast of bacon and eggs, watching the dawn come up the Thames from their exercise yard on the terrace? These overnight sessions take place during hotly contested Bills or policies, when the Opposition are determined to fight the Government every inch of the way, line by line, clause by clause. In such situations the sitting rule for 10.30 pm is suspended, to enable the debates to run for a few hours longer.

Despite the criticisms of cynics and rebels – and it is quite remarkable how Parliament affects even the wildest extremists until they become, as it were, fully House-trained – these old habits and procedures make sense and add to the tolerance, efficiency and humanity of modern Parliaments; because every tradition has a meaning and value of its own.

Volume 809
No. 66

Wednesday
20th January 1971

HOUSE OF COMMONS
OFFICIAL REPORT

PARLIAMENTARY
DEBATES
(HANSARD)

CONTENTS
TUESDAY 19th JANUARY 1971
[Continuation of Proceedings]

Industrial Relations Bill (Col. 445):
Considered in Committee

Armed Forces (Widows' Pensions):
Debate on Motion for Adjournment

WEDNESDAY 20th JANUARY 1971

Oral Answers to Questions:
Minister of Aviation Supply
Secretary of State for the Environment
Lord President of the Council

Post Office (Dispute):
Statement—[Mr. R. Carr]

Transport (London) Amendment:
Motion for leave to introduce Bill—[Mr. Spearing]—agreed to
Bill presented, and read the First time

European Economic Community:
Debate on Motion for Adjournment

Written Answers to Questions

LONDON
HER MAJESTY'S STATIONERY OFFICE
3s. 7d. [18p] net

The title cover of the Official Parliamentary Report, known as Hansard, which contains a verbatim report of the debates and proceedings of the Commons, and opposite is how the Ministers reply to the questions, and the supplementary questions which follow.

These traditions, tested by the centuries, help to strike the right balance between checking authoritarian Governments on the one hand, and, on the other, restraining and educating violent Oppositions who might otherwise paralyze the Parliamentary system by obstruction. This is the reality, and the system works extraordinarily well and efficiently.

It is often said that the Lower House no longer performs its critical function of keeping a Government in check and is unable under modern conditions effectively to control the Executive, which really means the Cabinet and the Civil Service. It is not the function of Parliament to govern, for that is the Government's responsibility, but to keep the Prime Minister and his Government under constant scrutiny and criticism; for Parliament is nothing if it is not the great forum, the assembly which mounts the national inquest and inquiry. When Parliament seems to fall down in these basic objectives it is not the fault of the system or procedures but more probably the fault of inadequate MPs, who, if not chosen by their constituency for their docility, are soon tamed by the power of the modern political party machines and Whips and by Governments exploiting power through the Cabinet system

HOUSE OF COMMONS

Wednesday, 20th January, 1971

The House met at half-past Two o'clock

PRAYERS

[Mr. SPEAKER *in the Chair*]

PRIVATE BUSINESS

PAISLEY CORPORATION (CART NAVIGATION) ORDER CONFIRMATION BILL

Mr. Gordon Campbell presented a Bill to confirm a Provisional Order under Section 7 of the Private Legislation Procedure (Scotland) Act, 1936, relating to Paisley Corporation (Cart Navigation).

To be considered upon Tuesday next and to be printed. [Bill 89.]

ORAL ANSWERS TO QUESTIONS

AVIATION SUPPLY

Aircraft Industry (Future Projects)

2. **Mr. Marten** asked the Minister of Aviation Supply if he will make a statement on future supersonic projects for the British aircraft industry.

The Minister of Aviation Supply (Mr. Frederick Corfield): I think that we must at this stage concentrate on making a success of Concorde.

Mr. Marten: I agree with the Minister in that profound statement, but could he say what research is going on for the next stage, that is, research into hypersonic flight?

Mr. Corfield: Very little at the present moment.

3. **Mr. Marten** asked the Minister of Aviation Supply if he will make a statement on future subsonic projects for the British aircraft industry.

Mr. Corfield: I take the Question to apply to civil projects. The Government are not responsible for finding projects for the industry; the initiative lies with the manufacturers. But I am prepared to consider any applications for Government launching aid.

Mr. Marten: What is being done by the industry to develop short take-off and landing aircraft, primarily in order to avoid congestion on the short air traffic routes?

Mr. Corfield: Several studies are in progress both in my Department and in the industry. We hope to be able to study these thoroughly in the next few weeks, but I do not think that there is much prospect of a project which will go into development in the near future.

Mr. Dalyell: Do these studies involve other European countries at present?

Mr. Corfield: Yes, Sir.

Aircraft Projects (Commercial Returns)

4. **Mr. Carter** asked the Minister of Aviation Supply what is the total of Government expenditure incurred since 1945 on civil aviation that failed to produce a commercial product.

Mr. Corfield: If the hon. Member is referring to aircraft which have failed to achieve any sales, about £40 million.

Mr. Carter: I thank the Minister for that reply. It is rather less than I thought it would be. But will he agree that what the aircraft industry requires today is a secure future based on feasible projects and that the recent cuts which the Government have made in the projected programmes of the British aircraft industry do not give much hope for that kind of prospect in the foreseeable future?

Mr. Corfield: Of course, the ideal would be a steady stream of viable projects. The hon. Gentleman refers to cuts. That is a rather odd way of describing a refusal to support with launching aid a project in relation to which there was a rival project of the same nature in which a British aircraft company was involved.

and treating Parliament as a rubber stamp. (See chapter 7 on Political Parties and power of the Whips.)

This illustrates the need to guard constantly the freedom and supreme independence of Parliament, no longer from autocratic Kings and power-hungry Lords and Barons and the excesses of the Feudal system, but from the new threat of Cabinet and Executive convenience; the endless challenge of bureaucratic encroachment. In 1929 Lord Hewart, then Lord Chief Justice, wrote a remarkable book, entitled *The New Despotism* which described the struggle in these terms:

> The old despotism, which is defeated, offered Parliament a challenge. The new despotism, which is not yet defeated, gives Parliament an anaesthetic. The strategy is different, but the goal is the same. It is to subordinate Parliament, to evade critics and to render the will or the caprice of the Executive unfettered and supreme.

The challenge changes, but the battle remains the same.

Leaving the public galleries, on the adjournment of the House, and moving through the Members' and Central lobbies towards the St. Stephen's exit, the visitor hears policemen on all sides shouting 'Who goes Home?' This cry dates back to those early days when Members of Parliament, sitting late, were anxious to travel home in company, in mutual protection against personal attacks from footpads and highwaymen.

It is an eerie experience as the lights are turned off to the point of semi-darkness to hear 'who goes home?', and one may sense the many generations of MPs who have made their contribution to the long spiritual and physical struggle for freedom, happiness and dignity against an endless succession and variety of dangers to them both from within the country and from abroad.

n THURSDAY, 26th November, the House will meet at 2.30 p.m.

ebate on a Motion to take note of the Consultative Document on the Industrial Relations Bill.

mportant divisions will take place and your attendance at 9.30 p.m. or 10.00 p.m. is essential.

n FRIDAY, 27th November, the House will meet at 11 a.m.

Private Members' Motions

he need for greater safety at sea. (Mr. Albert Costain)

he need for increasing the allocation of resources to the elderly in and out of Hospitals. (Dr. Tom Stuttaford)

he Population Problem. (Sir David Renton)

Your attendance is requested.

....

n Monday, 30th November, the House will meet at 2.30 p.m.

rivate Members' Motions until 7 p.m.

o call attention to a subject and to move a resolution. (Mr. A. Morris)

he need for a clear statement on development area policy. (Mr. E. Armstrong)

ontradictions in Government Fuel Policy. (Mr. R. Carter)

t 7 p.m., Family Income Supplements Bill: Report and 3rd Reading.

embers are asked to be ready to respond to a 2-line whip.

FRANCIS PYM

9.11.70

Examples of the imperative three-line Whip, the less compulsive two-liner, and the informative but more permissive single-liner reminder on business coming up.

CHAPTER 5

The Prime Minister

MELBOURNE *I think it a damned bore and I am in many minds what I should do.*

SECRETARY: *Why, damn it, such a position was never occupied by any Greek or Roman, and if it lasts only two months it is well worth while to have been Prime Minister of England.*

MELBOURNE: *By God, that's true. I'll go.*

In the end Lord Melbourne was Prime Minister for almost seven years, and ruled the Commons for twenty-five. He was the twenty-second of the forty-eight Prime Ministers who have held office since Sir Robert Walpole assumed power under the first of the Georges in 1721.

Today, after 250 years, many people complain that modern Prime Ministers have become too powerful, too Presidential, too autocratic in the personal power now concentrated in their hands. Most critics say they are too much like the American Presidents, who are a combination of elected monarchs and national political leaders voted to power on party tickets. What they mean by this comparison is that the British Prime Ministers have become too much like one-man governments on their own.

The comparison, however, is too superficial. Presidents can continue in power for their full term of four years, even when their policies are constantly repudiated and frustrated by their 'Parliament'. A British Prime Minister, on the other hand, would not last long if his major policies were always being defeated in the House of Commons. Under our system of Parliamentary democracy a Prime Minister derives his power and authority from the Commons, but exerts it through the Cabinet and Executive.

It all depends on the Prime Minister, of course. Of the Prime Ministers of this century, Lloyd George and Winston Churchill established complete personal power, the nearest to Parliamentary dictatorship this country has experienced since Oliver Cromwell. They came very close to the Presidential system in the sense of predominant one-man rule only when the country was fighting for survival in grave national emergencies. Parliament was prepared to surrender power to the wartime leaders, an act which would never have been contemplated in peace time.

Other Prime Ministers, cast in less commanding stature, saw their role chiefly as chairmen of the Cabinet – like Attlee, Bonar Law and Baldwin. Harold Macmillan, at the height of his powers, totally dominated his Government, and so complete and unquestioned was his supremacy as 'Supermac' that he was able to carry off the dismissal of seven Cabinet Ministers in one night.

Constitutionally, the Prime Minister is *primus inter pares*, the first among equals. Or, as Lord Morley saw it, 'the Prime Minister is the cornerstone of the arch.' The principle of equality goes back a very long time, to Sir Robert Walpone who first set the role in 1721. When the Hanoverians came to the throne, George I broke the procedure observed by all the earlier Kings, who had presided over their Councils or Assemblies or Governments in person in order more often than not to ensure that they got their own way, especially in obtaining the money they wanted. The first of the Georges found the

English procedures and language difficult to understand, so he invited Walpole to preside over his inner Council or Cabinet.

That started it. From Walpole we date not merely the status and power of the Prime Minister, but also the Cabinet system as we know it today. Before then Ministers acted independently on behalf of the Crown, and had no shared interest. Walpole and his successors established the collective role of Ministers in Cabinet. And, in consequence, the party system was born. As the Prime Minister, his Cabinet, Government and the majority system in Parliament developed in power, Kings were pressurized to retreat until they reconciled themselves to the role of Constitutional Monarchy. Now the Sovereign reigns but no longer rules.

The Prime Minister, as the Queen's principal ministerial adviser, holds the highest office open to her subjects by virtue of her invitation to him to form a Government. He is invited to do so not because the Sovereign prefers him to all other rivals but invariably and traditionally because he is the leader of the majority party in Parliament, the situation arising after a General Election. In all but the most exceptional circumstances, she invites him to become her First Minister because she is advised that he has the best chance of getting a majority of the House of Commons to support him and his Administration.

His official title is also that of First Lord of the Treasury.

When a Prime Minister forms his Government, he starts with the Cabinet, which in recent years and under different parties has included between eighteen and twenty-two Ministers, the great majority of whom become heads of the major Departments of State and other Ministries. According to historical precedent and tradition, Cabinets are sub-committees of the Privy Council: all

Cabinet Ministers become 'Right Honourable Gentlemen', the courtesy recognition of their membership of the Privy Council. Today, of course, the Cabinet is the supreme authority in the power pyramid, and long ago outgrew its role as a subsidiary of the Council. But, because of the extent of a Prime Minister's patronage, Ministers' first loyalty is to him. He is the boss who hires and fires. Normally a Prime Minister can be overthrown only if there is a majority of the Cabinet grouped against him and determined to replace him by one of their number. Prime Ministers of all parties, however, have a high survival ratio, and insurance brokers would rate their prospects of longevity at No. 10, Downing Street, measured against the normal political hazards of their trade, as excellent.

The Prime Minister and his Cabinet form the Executive, in conjunction with the Civil Service, and is the supreme party political vehicle for translating Government and party policies into legislation, in the form of Bills which, when passed by both Houses of Parliament, become Acts and are added to the statute book. As Sir Ivor Jennings so aptly describes the constitutional power structure, the Cabinet is the core of the British constitutional system. In short, the country is ruled by a modern system of Cabinet Government, increasingly overtaking and displacing the old traditions of Parliamentary Government.

What happens when a Prime Minister dies suddenly, or is overthrown by a secret coup, before the party's plans for the succession are completed? Clearly, the Queen's Government must be carried on, without interruption, and as the two major parties now elect their leader by popular vote of their Parliamentary parties, the procedure is much simpler than it used to be.

Party leaders are democratically elected by their MPs.

In the Conservative party the older, traditional method of selection enabled the leader to emerge after a complex system of soundings among MPs and Peers, the constituency leaders and the party organization. This system of selection by what a former Conservative Minister and Party Chairman, the late Mr. Iain Macleod, described as 'the magic circle', was discarded a few years ago. Now Party leaders, as prospective Prime Ministers, are popularly elected by their Parliamentary Parties acting as electoral colleges.

In the old days, before the rigid party organizations of the present time, Prime Ministers were very often selected by the Crown. But today this would be undesirable, because it would involve the monarchy in party politics if the Queen were to invite someone to form the new Government who was not likely to become the party leader, nor certain to have a Parliamentary majority behind him. While the situation has not yet arisen, the expert view is that a Deputy Leader or Deputy Prime Minister or the most senior Minister in the Cabinet as the elder statesman (because the title of Deputy Prime Minister is unknown in the Constitution) would preside over the Government until the majority party had an opportunity to elect a new leader.

One further reason why a Prime Minister is nowadays regarded as exercising Presidential powers, is that he is so powerful in so many fields: he is the Queen's principal Minister, he is the complete master of his Cabinet whose members owe their coveted status to his patronage and he can appoint, sack, promote or demote them at will; he has all the Government, Parliamentary and Party levers of powers in his grip; he is party leader and boss of the party organization; and in addition to keeping all this network of modern power in his personal control, he is inevitably the best known national figure because of his constant exposure to, and expertise in, the modern communications media like television, radio and newspapers.

Prime Ministers, as we have seen, are difficult to sack or defeat (party leaders in Opposition are much more easily displaced). Asquith in 1916, during the First World War, was the last Prime Minister to be overthrown by a combined Cabinet and party revolt – the eclipse of Lloyd George in 1922 was due to the breakup of the Coalition of parties supporting his Government. But apart from them, the succession of Prime Ministers produces a remarkably similar pattern. Bonar Law was overtaken by a fatal illness; Baldwin was unique in that he survived more party revolts than others and in the end retired at a time and in the circumstances selected by himself months in advance; Ramsay MacDonald left the Premiership because of failing health, Neville Chamberlain was compelled to resign because of the collapse of his policies and a revolt inside the Parliamentary Conservative party though not in the Cabinet; Sir Winston Churchill resigned because of his great age; Sir Anthony Eden went because of his collapse in health, as did his successor, Harold Macmillan, after a serious operation; and Harold Wilson moved over to become Opposition leader on losing the 1970 general election.

A successful Prime Minister must be a combination of statesman, Parliamentarian, party manager and national leader, as well as being capable of being projected on television in popular modern terms. This may seem an odd test to apply, but it is impossible to imagine any party electing a leader who would be incompetent in front of the cameras, any more than they may be seen electing someone who would be hopeless on the platform before a mass audience: personality in mass media techniques counts for a great deal nowadays. Most important, he must be a captain of men, a natural leader of a team and a good administrator. He must also be a good butcher, never squeamish in ruthlessly sacking near and dear colleagues when their sacrifice serves the interests of Government and Party. Harold Macmillan, as we know, sacked no fewer than seven Cabinet Ministers in one quick, unhesitant purge, in his 'night of the long knives'.

In addition, the Prime Minister disposes of enormous patronage, not confined by any means to the twice-yearly Honours List which includes a formidable list of political honours from Peerages to the minor civil awards. In Government terms his patronage is widespread; altogether over ninety Ministers, ranging from Cabinet Ministers, through Ministers of State, Under-Secretaries, and Parliamentary Secretaries down to Junior Whips, owe their inclusion in the modern Government to the Prime Minister's selection; they owe their eminence and future survival to him; and in a party dispute over policies or personalities, their first loyalty is to him. The size of this pay-roll vote of over ninety, plus the army of unpaid Parliamentary Private Secretaries totalling some thirty or so, provides any Prime Minister with a solid base of personal support from which he can confidently face party political storms which threaten to overwhelm him. And if he is a shrewd party manager as well, in the tradition of Stanley Baldwin, Harold Macmillan and Harold Wilson, each of whom knew how to combine Prime Ministerial power with tough control of their parties, his position is almost impregnable.

CHAPTER 6

How the Cabinet works

On Tuesday and Thursday mornings, around 10.30 am, there is great activity in Downing Street. In the space of a few minutes a succession of official cars draw up at the door of No. 10 and the policemen and attendants admit about a score of men and one woman (it is odd how it has always been one, with only two for an exceptionally short period of a few months, on the theory perhaps that one is enough and two is too many). Photographers are always there in periods of crisis, and the crowd of onlookers on the pavement opposite, in front of the Foreign Office quadrangle, try to recognize the faces.

This burst of activity means that the Cabinet is in session. The Cabinet is the premier instrument of government in this country, the supreme authority which links the Crown, Parliament, Government and the Executive; it represents the most powerful group of people in our national life. The meetings are usually held twice a week, lasting normally until almost one o'clock, although they are held more often during periods of Government, policy or personal crises, or emergency situations at home or abroad when, of course, groups of Ministers are more or less in continuous session. In addition, meetings of various Cabinet Sub-Committees and Ministerial groups are held daily; the Prime Minister himself presides over the major ones dealing with defence, foreign, economic and other major policies; while the others, in more specialized groups, meet in the Palace of Westminster or in the Departments in Whitehall mainly concerned.

Let us enter and see what goes on inside. There is a square hall or largish vestibule immediately inside the front door of No. 10, leading to a corridor which runs straight to the heart of the building. At the far end you will notice a row of hat and coat pegs, identified not by individual names but by the offices of Cabinet Ministers – Chancellor of the Exchequer, Home Secretary and so on: a reminder that the office, not the Minister, endures—a warning of the transitory nature of political power.

A few minutes before the Cabinet meeting starts at 10.30 am Ministers gather in the small ante-room, where they chat, gossip and exchange views on current topics, calling each other by their first names. But this relaxed, informality soon disappears when the double doors swing open and Ministers are invited to join the Prime Minister in the Cabinet room. Then they are on official parade. The Tom, Dick and Harry familiarity of a few seconds before is replaced by protocol, and Ministers are referred to, not by name, but by their Deparmtents. 'I agree with what the Home Secretary has just said'; 'the Foreign Secretary has not convinced me on this one'; 'I am very much opposed to the Minister of Transport's plans and my Department feels strongly about the implications.'

On this formal level, Ministers preface their opening sentences with a respectful 'Prime Minister, I would like to say . . .' thus acknowledging the primacy of the Prime Minister – and throughout the meeting Ministers address the Cabinet through him.

Cabinet Ministers are encouraged to be brief: if they were to take say five minutes each on a major issue occupying number one item on the agenda it would be nearly lunchtime before it could be settled. And for most meetings the agenda usually runs to ten or twelve items. As Lloyd George said: 'A man who makes a five-minute speech in Cabinet is voted a bore straightaway.'

Smoking is also strongly discouraged by most Prime Ministers but not prohibited; pipe-smoking Attlee permitted it, pipe-smoking Wilson permitted it within reason, non-smoker Heath strongly frowns on thc habit. For centuries, and in all Cabinets, the habit has persisted of Ministers scribbling notes and passing them to colleagues round the table; some of these come in handy for the subsequent memoirs which often help to provide for old age. Some of these passing notes have even been known to offer betting odds on how long a colleague would take to ride his hobby horse or how long another Minister would take to show his hand for or against a difficult problem.

The Cabinet room itself is large, high and solid, spacious in the grand eighteenth-century style of space, and has one of the finest views in London, overlooking Horse Guards and St. James's Park. The Cabinet table, covered in blue cloth, strikes the visitor as impressively long and broad. The Prime Minister sits not at the head or end of the table, but in the centre, halfway down the side immediately in front of the fireplace and below the portrait of Walpole, the first Prime Minister.

The seating arrangements, you will notice, are governed by seniority and protocol; next to the Prime Minister, on his right, is the Secretary of the Cabinet, opposite him the Deputy Prime Minister (if the title is used at the particular time, though it is unknown to the constitution, being purely courtesy in acknowledging a party title like that of Deputy Leader): on his left is the Chancellor opposite the Foreign Secretary, sitting next to the Lord Chancellor; then to right and left the next most senior ranking Ministers, with the others tapering off according to the pecking order, known as the 'seniority list' which is determined when the Prime Minister makes his Cabinet appointments. There are a few additional places in reserve for those Ministers, usually in charge of Departments and known as Ministers of senior rating but outside the magic circle of Cabinet, who are invited to attend because policies or decisions affecting their Departments are on the agenda. They wait in the ante-room until their specialized subjects are reached; they sit in only during the discussion on their departmental affairs, then withdraw.

Although experts on the Constitution have written many volumes on the importance of the Cabinet system in principle and practice, very little is known of what really goes on inside, because even insiders are inhibited by their Privy Council oath from giving away too much in their memoirs (which have, in any case, to be approved by the Cabinet Secretary because of the need to preserve state security and official secrets). The meetings of the Cabinet are not only secret in theory, but secret in practice; historians have to wait thirty years before Cabinet minutes and Cabinet papers are available for inspection at the Public Records Office. Even Ministers are discouraged from taking notes during meetings, although judging from the series of memoirs and autobiographies of recent years, some Ministers are obviously blessed with better memories than others, or perhaps with better and fuller diaries written up at bed-time to aid instant recall later. The value of these private records for subsequent book and serialization rights is considerable.

Some Cabinets are more talkative, even loquacious, than

others, and for proof one can compare the minutes of Cabinet meetings as they become available many years later. Brevity and clarity are essential qualities among Cabinet Ministers, otherwise sessions would continue endlessly. There is the story of one Minister who went on and on in an impressive academic recital of the pros and cons; as the end of his performance seemed still far off the Prime Minister of the day – Attlee – intervened sharply, when the Minister paused for breath. 'Yes, very good, but we're still waiting for one of two very short words: Yes or No.'

The official theory is that all Cabinet decisions must be unanimous. This is not so; it is one of the myths carefully nurtured, but it is an essential myth nevertheless for the unity and continuity of Governments and parties, which would otherwise be over-strained by internal divisions. It is inconceivable that twenty or so Ministers should hold identical views on highly controversial subjects and policies and that they should all say and think the same round the table – for that would be the unanimity of the graveyard, as Aneurin Bevan said on another occasion. Inevitably almost unbridgeable differences develop in Cabinet discussions. In the end the Prime Minister sums up the discussion, expressing the sense of the meeting, and only on major issues of great importance, when Ministers on each side of the argument feel passionately, has he to start counting noses.

Another myth is that the Prime Minister never calls for a vote at Cabinet meetings. Records throughout history – and the Cabinet system has been going for 250 years – confirm the narrowness of majority decisions. On really big or grave issues the Prime Minister goes round the table, inviting each Minister in turn to express his opinions for or against a particular proposal, and in this way he can assess the strength of the two sides accurately, much more effectively than by a show of hands; and in his final summing up he can then take account of the shading of opinion among his Ministers. Of course, all such factors are influenced by the basic unity which must exist inside the Cabinet.

Cabinet Ministers are well briefed in advance on all subjects appearing on the agenda, which is prepared by the Cabinet Secretary in consultation with the Prime Minister; by these methods they present their own and their departmental views and policies to full Cabinet meetings in advance and often to Cabinet Committees as well, and thereby save precious time later in spelling out details. These official papers and documents are circulated in those red and green hard despatch boxes which you may see going in and out of No. 10 Downing Street and all Government departments at all hours. All top secret, top security papers and reports are distributed day and night on a shuttle service, prepared by the Cabinet Secretariat. Only Ministers are able to open these despatch boxes with specially cut keys which they must always carry on their person. If one key is lost, the locks are changed and new keys are cut by the locksmiths. The secrets are well protected; all Cabinet Ministers are members of the Privy Council – this explains their official courtesy designation as 'Right Honourable' – and take the oath of secrecy.

There is no constitutional maximum or minimum number of Ministers in a Cabinet, and the total varies according to the decisions of Prime Ministers – usually between eighteen and twenty-three. Ministers are in the Cabinet because they are appointed to great Departments of State, like the Treasury, Home Office and so on, although there are a few non-departmental or sinecure posts, like Lord President of the Council, Lord Privy Seal, Minister without Portfolio, or Chancellor of the Duchy of Lancaster. They are officially appointed by the Queen, constitutionally on the advice of her Prime Minister; they are received in Privy Council audience, and kiss hands when they get their seals of office from the sovereign. Usually about eighteen or nineteen members of the Cabinet are MPs who sit in the Commons; only three or four are Peers from the House of Lords.

The Cabinet takes all major and important policy decisions of Government although sometimes within Departments decisions are taken by senior Civil Servants in the name of the Ministers, who are responsible in political and Parliamentary terms for all actions taken on their behalf by anonymous officials.

The famous authority, Walter Bagehot, wrote over a hundred years ago, and his wisdom is just as relevant today, that the 'Cabinet is a combining committee, a hyphen which joins, a buckle which fastens, the Legislative part of the State to the Executive part of the State'.

It would be impossible for the modern Cabinet system to function efficiently, or a Government to survive, without the well-established tradition of collective Cabinet responsibility, applying to all Ministers. 'It doesn't matter what we say, so long as we all say the same', as one Prime Minister put it. This means in practice that no matter how deep the disagreements or arguments, or even the strength of majority and minority votes in the Cabinet during the discussions round the table, when the Cabinet reaches a conclusion the system demands that all Ministers must loyally subscribe to and support by speech and vote the decisions reached; they must not contract out from their liability and loyalty to the doctrine of collective responsibility. If any Minister feels so strongly about the subject, and cannot accept the Cabinet decision in conscience and honour, then his duty is to resign his office.

The only occasion when the tradition of collective responsibility was breached was in the National Government in 1932 under Ramsay MacDonald. Because this was a coalition of leaders of three parties, it was impossible to secure total agreement on proposals involving the old dispute between Protection and Free Trade. The experiment was then tried of Ministers in the Cabinet, representing three parties, adopting the extraordinary expedient of 'agreeing to differ' in order to allow three or four dissident Ministers to speak and vote in the House of Commons against the Cabinet's proposals. This was such a ridiculous compromise that it broke down very quickly, resulting in the dissenting Ministers resigning from the Government.

However far you look, you will not find any reference to the rôle and responsibility of the Cabinet in any of the constitutional statutes, though its existence is acknowledged often enough in Prime Ministerial announcements of new appointments. This is a notable example of the effectiveness of the British unwritten Constitution, because here is the supreme authority, the most powerful group of people in the nation, exerting almost limitless power, yet without any precise definition of what it is and what it can do. Yet it lies at the very heart of the complex system of government and administration. Sir Ivor Jennings defined the Cabinet as the core of the British constitutional system. It is the supreme directing authority. It provides unity to the British system of government. Yet there is no legal authority defining its existence.

The Cabinet, which, as explained earlier, started out as a Committee of the Privy Council, used to be the main instrument of the Crown's power, and was formed in those early days by the most senior, influential and powerful members of the Court's circle. In due course, the more select of these became, in turn, the most trusted advisers and met under the King's chairmanship. The system of cabals started creating its own inner cabals, just as inner Cabinets today exert the real power, in much the same way as the inner War Cabinets formed by Lloyd George and Churchill assumed the central direction and decision making. The word 'cabal' dates back to James I, when his inner circle of trusties became known as the King's Cabal – the word formed by the first letters of their surnames.

The early development of the Cabinet system was encouraged by the first two King Georges' difficulties with English; in view of their greater interest in the affairs of their native Hanover than of their adopted England they delegated the job of chairing the Cabinet to their Prime Minister. From the first Hanoverians sprung the Prime Ministerial, Cabinet, and the party systems, starting from the time of Sir Robert Walpole. No wonder that Walpole's portrait has pride of place in No. 10 Downing Street's art gallery of Prime Ministers!

At the same time began the doctrine of collective responsibility referred to earlier in this chapter. Before then Ministers owed their direct allegiance to the King, and had no common links or loyalties to other Ministers. Each one stood alone, in his own sector of responsibility. But immediately the Cabinet system became established as the central arch in Government and Parliament, creating the party system in consequence, Ministers were no longer obliged to function in isolation, disassociating themselves if need be from decisions of other Ministers, but instead acquired a common identity and loyalty. In broad terms, this development meant, as they say in trade union terms, one in – all in, one out – all out. This started to tilt the balance of power away from Parliament to the Cabinet and the Executive, and this trend has gone on unchecked ever since.

Today all the executive power for governing the country, running the apparatus of power, administering the great affairs of state, is concentrated in and comes from the Cabinet. In day-to-day practice, in our modern system of Parliamentary democracy geared to the two-party system, Ministers owe their personal and collective loyalty to the Prime Minister, who in turn depends upon Parliament, and its majority system for the overall support of his Government; just as Government and Parliament consisting of individual MPs, depend in the final analysis upon public opinion and popular franchise for their election and survival. At the centre of this complex and sensitive power structure is the Prime Minister who can dominate his Cabinet, Government and Parliament by the formidable mechanisms and levers of power which he alone controls; yet in personal terms he must retain the confidence of Cabinet, Government, Parliament and Party if he is to remain in power for long. By many tests a dominant Prime Minister deploys more personal power than an American President.

In short, it is a unique system peculiar to the British tradition of government and way of life, but difficult to understand because of its contradictions and paradoxes. For instance, as Dr. Eric Taylor says in his highly professional study of the more technical aspects of Parliamentary procedure, 'it (the Cabinet) is chosen secretly, and appointed by one man, the Prime Minister, who does not consult the House of Commons about any of his nominees. The proceedings of the Cabinet are still a close secret, even to the House of Commons; it has no dealings with the House of Commons as a body; it has no organic connection with it. It allocates its functions to itself.'

The Cabinet system works with astonishing success, incorporating the wisdom and experience of many centuries. It is about the most efficient power system in democratic government. Yet there is no written rule book available. Instinct, tradition, continuity, the experience of many centuries – these are the qualities which provide the secret. It has no legal existence, yet it works with impressive efficiency. As Quintin Hogg says, in *The Purpose of Parliament*: 'In general, one can say that in peace-time the Cabinet is the instrument by which Britain in governed, subject only to the support of a House of Commons elected by the people.'

The balance between a Prime Minister and his Cabinet clearly varies from Government to Government, according to the relationship between the Premier and his Ministers. There is argument between the constitutional experts about whether Britain is ruled today by a Prime Ministerial (or near-Presidential) form of government or by a collective Cabinet system of government. In a recently published volume on the working of the Cabinet, Patrick Gordon Walker, who served in Cabinets under two Prime Ministers, Attlee and Wilson, argued that it is the Cabinet system which prevails, and in support instanced three occasions when Harold Wilson was over-ruled by his Cabinet.

On the other hand, Richard Crossman, an equally experienced Minister, contended in his famous introduction to Bagehot's *The English Constitution* (an argument developed more recently in his Godkin lectures at Harvard), that it is Prime Ministerial power bordering on the Presidential which prevails. The commonsense view of these constitutional arguments is that it all depends on the extent to which a Prime Minister overshadows his Ministers, and has the character and personality to dominate them – the test varies from Government to Government. A recent biography recalls how Baldwin decided to overrule the views of his entire Cabinet and go his own way over his 'peace in our time' policy on trade unions, with notable personal success.

There is also the case of how Asquith as Prime Minister pushed through Lloyd George's controversial People's Budget in 1909 (which laid the foundations of the health service) when a vote in the Cabinet would have seen it decisively rejected. As Lloyd George himself recalled: 'They were all against it and they all said so; and then Asquith rubbed his chin and said "I think the balance of argument is in favour" and put it through.' That is a good example of how Prime Ministerial Government worked sixty and more years ago, with lessons in the exercise of power which one feels sure have not gone unnoticed by Mr. Edward Heath, who is already identified by some commentators as developing Prime Ministerial rule, completely overshadowing his Cabinet colleagues.

On balance, there can be little doubt that this country is moving towards Prime Ministerial Government and away from Cabinet Government, due to the personal control exerted from No. 10 Downing Street over the vast modern apparatus of centralized power manipulated by the Prime Minister, who has at his command the highly geared Cabinet Secretariat, the massive power of the Civil Service and his personal authority over the Parliamentary party and the party machine.

One of the best descriptions of the Cabinet system, and of the manner in which the influence of Parliament has been eroded by the Executive, was given by

L. S. Amery, himself an experienced Minister, in his *Thoughts on the Constitution.*

> 'The central directing instrument of government, in legislation as well as in administration, is the Cabinet. It is in Cabinet that administrative action is co-ordinated and that legislative proposals are sanctioned. It is the Cabinet which controls Parliament and governs the country. In no other country is there such a concentration of power and such a capacity for decisive action as that possessed by a British Cabinet, provided always that it enjoys the support of a majority in the House of Commons.'

On this theme of Parliamentary Government being replaced first by Cabinet Government and now by Prime Ministerial Government, Christopher Hollis, a former MP, in his book *Can Parliament Survive?* poses the question whether power, in the next phase, may not pass wholly out of the hands of those nominally responsible for it into a new form of 'managerial Government'. This sobering thought may prove to be the new style of Government developing for the future, in harmony with the modern management techniques in administration and confirmed by recent experiments in importing 'tycoons' from big business into the Whitehall structure of the Civil Service.

CHAPTER 7

How the Party System works

I always voted at my Party's call
And never thought of thinking for myself at all.
W. S. Gilbert

It is a noble ambition to be a Member of Parliament and a most honourable calling, because there can be few worthier careers than one dedicated to public service. There may be a few opportunists in the Westminster community; but you will find that MPs of all parties in the mass are inspired by a sense of duty and maintain very high standards of honour and integrity.

That critics deride 'party politics' as though they were squalid and disreputable may be due to the fact that party politics and party politicians seldom get a good Press. This is partly because of the salutary Love-Hate relationship which has existed between the two estates for many years, and also because of the experienced Parliamentary correspondents' cool appraisal of sometimes heated and undignified events. Disillusion expressed about politics in general is often really concerned with disagreement with, and opposition to, policies of a particular Government. Even so, the fact has to be recognized that many people do become disillusioned and cynical over party politics, but unfairly so; and the mood more often than not reflects a temporary feeling of frustration and discontent expressed in Poujadist protest.

Nowadays, to become an MP, one must belong to one of the parties. There have been many famous independent non-party MPs throughout the years, who made outstanding contributions to the House of Commons, but those days have long since gone. The way of the independent, like that of the transgressor, was always hard: 'An independent Member of Parliament is a Member of Parliament who cannot be depended upon' was the famous poisoned barb written to Queen Victoria by the fourteenth Earl of Derby. The scales were weighted against the independents even then.

The chance of any candidate, however distinguished, standing as an independent against the major parties and being elected is now so remote as to be non-existent. The last group of Independent Members represented the Universities, but when the fifteen University seats were abolished by the Attlee Government in 1948 it marked the end of the independent tradition in politics. You will not get far if you opt to be an independent candidate today, because more likely than not you will lose your deposit of £150 and never again be heard of politically.

We are now in the age of mass, monolithic, centrally organized parties, and because they cover such a wide political front they have really become organized coalitions within themselves. On some issues the Left-wing of the Conservative party and Right-wing of the Labour party often find themselves closer together than do the Right and Left within each party. It is now widely recognized that the stability of Parliament and of our democratic system of Government depends upon the strength of the party system; you will notice that whenever a party is gripped by internal tensions and disunity the disagreements set up unhealthy reactions in the Commons and spread confusion and delay. A strong and healthy party system is a precondition for a vigorous dispatch of public business.

There is no specific mention of parties as such in the constitutional laws and Parliamentary procedures. The nearest these have come to recognizing their existence was in the recent electoral law reforms which provided that candidates may be identified by their party labels on the ballot papers – the first time the party system has been recognized by law.

When a prospective Prime Minister receives the Royal Commission to try to form a Government he is selected for this duty not because he happens to be the leader of the victorious party – which is the truth – but, technically, because he is considered most likely to be able to command a majority in Parliament.

This protocol comes down from the days when loyalties and majorities were much more fluid and movable than they are today. Less than a century ago MPs were constantly changing between parties and governments, according to the big issues of the hour, far removed from the rigid, oligarchic party organizations of today with their whipping arrangements and harsh disciplines. In the nineteenth century, and earlier, the large numbers of independent MPs, and even party MPs with loyalties far freer and easier than today, were able to make and unmake Governments by moving spontaneously across the no-man's-land in the middle, creating as it were a mobile consensus. Now the reality is that Governments and Cabinets could not continue in office with reasonable prospects of stability and survival, if they could not count upon the support of majority parties in Parliament.

Party leaders and the Whips have a habit of laying down

the law about the likelihood of party disaster and political chaos if rebels push their revolts against the party line too far, but despite the scare tactics and the shrill headlines, a Prime Minister is seldom overthrown by the breakdown of loyalty and discipline within his party.

The party system first started to develop in the reigns of Charles I and Charles II, although some historians claim that the origins must be traced earlier to the Reformation. In the constant struggles for ascendancy and power between Kings, Governments, and Parliaments the Tory party became the centre of attraction for the Barons, squires and religious leaders; hence the traditional cry of the Conservatives: 'For King, Country and Church'. Religion was a potent factor in shaping early political loyalties, notably in the reign of Charles I, when people divided into Royalist versus Parliamentary supporters according to their views about the thirty-nine Articles in the prayer book. In due course the rival movements, known as the Court and Country groups of Roundheads and Cavaliers, developed into the embryo Whig and Tory parties. Opposing the Tories were the Whigs, the new race of landlords and commercial leaders starting to found and develop firms, industries and new enterprises, who were quick to align themselves with popular pressures for the representation of the new interests.

Ministers were appointed by the King, hence their loyalties were then to the Crown in personal and independent terms and not collectively to the Prime Minister and Cabinet of the day; and because of this royal patronage most Governments prior to 1715 were heterogeneous collections of individuals with firmly independent personalities, more like the all-party coalitions we have had occasionally in this century – twice in the two World Wars and once in a serious national emergency.

It was in 1681 that the two parties were first mentioned, and both started as terms of abuse. The Duke of York's supporters, mostly Catholics, were derided by their opponents as Tories, the word originally given to the raiding and lawless Irish bog-trotters. As for the Whigs, their description came from the Scottish Covenanters, or Whiggamores, shortened to Whigs. Religious pressures were also strong: the Tories favourable to the High Church, the Whigs leaning towards the Protestant cause. The influence of religious beliefs upon the early growth of party alignments is worth noting, because 300 years later Morgan Phillips, Secretary of the Labour Party, claimed that the creation and development of Labour as a movement owed more to Methodism than to Marxism.

The party system got its first outline from Sir Robert Walpole, who formed his Government in 1715 and pioneered the system of having all his Ministers from the same party. Thus four main features started to emerge more or less simultaneously under Walpole:

1. The Cabinet formed from one party;
2. The first guidelines for the party system itself, in order to support the one-party Government;
3. The principle of collective responsibility among Ministers; and
4. The first major electoral development of making Governments and parties accountable to the popular will of the constituencies (admittedly on a limited and selective franchise then).

Thus we see the start of a delicate interlocking of self-interest and power, each in turn linked with the three others, a basic system of interdependence for ensuring stability, continuity and efficient administration.

Despite its contradictions and weaknesses, the party system works with remarkable efficiency and stability; and without this solid foundation of power, Parliament as well as the Government would soon be reduced to impotence and chaos, creating on the one hand the danger of coups, cabals and pacts between ever-changing groups and cliques and, on the other, the danger of permanent dictatorship. If you doubt this, consider what happens in overseas Parliaments containing large numbers of overlapping groups, where crises often continue for months, sometimes years (as in Italy in recent memory) because of the difficulty in forming stable coalition governments from constantly changing alliances.

Two authoritative views are worth quoting here to sum up the value and meaning of the two-party system: First, Disraeli: 'I say you can have no Parliamentary Government if you have no Party Government; and therefore when gentlemen denounce Party Government they strike at that scheme of Government which in my opinion has made this country great and which, I hope, will keep it great'. More recently, Quintin Hogg wrote: 'The truth is that Party is as vital a political institution in this country as Parliament; without Party, Parliament would wither and decline into a debating club without responsibility, or a Reichstag whose business it would be to register approval of the decisions of a dictator or a bureaucracy.' And what binds parties together? Edmund Burke's answer was: 'A party is a body of men united for promoting, by their joint endeavours, the national interest upon some particular principle in which they are all agreed.'

An account of the modern two-party system is given by Richard Crossman in his Introduction to Bagehot's *The English Constitution*. After making the point about how the former independence of private MPs gave the

Commons its collective character and provided the most effective check on the Executive, he explains:

> 'Now the prime responsibility of the Member is no longer to his conscience or to the elector, but to his party. Without accepting the discipline of the party he cannot be elected; and, if he defies that discipline, he risks political death. Even forty years ago it was still possible to cross the floor and survive. But today the Member who loses the Whip may win the next election, but after that the party machine will destroy him. Party loyalty has become the prime political virtue required of an MP, and the test of that loyalty is his willingness to support the official leadership when he knows it to be wrong.'

The moral is that a rebel has no future when in conflict with his party, for the Whips – the name derives from the old whippers-in of the hunting field – have no compunction in threatening and imposing discipline, leading in extreme cases of revolt to expulsion, in order to protect the interests of the leadership, Government and especially the party.

This is the side of party organization which perhaps causes the greatest cynicism outside, leading to the gives and sneers about MPs being lobby 'fodder', marching faithfully through the division lobbies at the orders of a three-line whip, like so many docile sheep safely penned by collie dogs. Indeed Christopher Hollis suggested in his book *Can Parliament Survive?* that it would be simpler and more economic to keep a flock of tame sheep and drive them through the lobby in appropriate numbers.

When the parting of the ways is finally reached, a rebel MP outside the party soon discovers he faces political oblivion. In the case of the Labour party, his political crimes in defying the party line are reported to the National

Executive, who, failing a statement of repentance and recantation, have the power to expel the Member from membership of the party (but not from membership of the House of Commons, for only the voters can do that. In any case however, his days are numbered). In the Conservative party, persistent defiance and indiscipline is noted by the Constituency Association, who exercise their freedom to adopt another candidate at the next general election in specially difficult situations.

The lesson is, according to Disraeli: 'Damn your principles: stick to your party.'

One consequence of the sweeping powers vested in the party machines is that major decisions are transferred from the floor of the House of Commons to the private party meetings in committee rooms upstairs. There the critical and rebellious MPs are able to let off steam and express their most vigorous opposition to their leaders in the presence of their Parliamentary colleagues, but once the policy decisions are reached, they are expected to go along with the majority – and to control their revolt if possible without damaging party unity in the Chamber.

Meetings of the full Parliamentary parties and of specialist groups and committees of the party MPs are held every week at Westminster, to discuss policies, problems and the large and small questions of the hour among themselves. Such meetings not only help the parties to form reasonably united views and lines of debate, but they also serve as useful barometers for leaders and whips to discover when new trends and perhaps anxieties are working through the ranks.

Without central and cohesive organization of large parties, however, it is obvious that modern Parliaments would soon be paralyzed, with Governments finding themselves unable to get their policies and measures through. Whereas voters used to elect Members of Parliament the majority of whom were Independents, or at least independent-minded Members, now they in effect elect the Prime Minister and Government by deciding between the party candidates, a subtle development which accounts for the autocratic powers of the whips in underpinning the power structure and dominance of the party machine.

Robert McKenzie, in his book *British Political Parties*, sees the role of the MP within the party machine in this way: 'Setting aside the party myths and the inter-party propaganda, it is clear that the primary function of the mass organizations of the Conservative and Labour parties is to sustain two competing leaders between whom the electorate as a whole may periodically choose.'

But if the Independent MPs and candidates have been overwhelmed by the party organizations, so also have the 'carpet-baggers', the name given to candidates who used to arrive in constituencies where vacancies were pending, carrying only the old-fashioned carpet-bags with their clothes, in a kind of smash-and-grab exercise for the nomination. They too have gone, because it has become impossible (except for local 'favourite sons') for candidates to make the constituency short list unless on the approved panel at the central headquarters of their parties. When a constituency association is on the look-out for a new candidate, the High Commands usually provide a variety of names from the approved list, to be supplemented if necessary by a few worthy local figures.

Westminster used to be famous for its gifted amateurs among the MPs of all parties. Now it is the age of professionals, mostly full-time, with only a few professions or occupations remaining like the law, public relations, advertising and journalism, where it is possible to combine private careers and private incomes, with Parliamentary life.

The types of MPs have been changing in step with the changes in the character of the parties: the contemporary Conservative, Labour and Liberal parties are completely different from their prewar predecessors and the same is true of their MPs. In the Labour party, the traditional working class Members, with Keir Hardie cloth caps and from trade union and elementary school backgrounds, have been overtaken by the new generation of educated professionals, just as in the Conservative party the old squirearchy, the famous titled and landed families, the captains of industry, have been largely displaced by the new professionals, managers and technocrats. The former class identities of parties have almost gone too. But however much they change, the parties continue the political and power battles which have not altered much in tactics and methods over the years, although the old issues have been replaced by new ones; they are still engaged, as Froude said in his life of Disraeli, in a form of 'concealed civil war'. Quintin Hogg, in his book quoted earlier, disagrees with this verdict and argues that the party system is a substitute for civil war.

The role of the parties enables the country to choose mainly between two alternatives, between two programmes, between the Government and the alternative Government, and perhaps the most crucial choice of all, between the Prime Minister and the alternative Prime Minister – this is the near-Presidential judgment which decides most General Elections.

'A good party man', said Winston Churchill, when paying tribute to a colleague, Kingsley Wood, who had just died, 'is one who puts his party above himself, his country above his party'.

The channel of power operates from the Prime Minister and his Cabinet – and on the other side from the Opposition Leader and his 'Shadow' Cabinet – through the Parliamentary parties (which elect their leaders by popular vote) to the party organizations outside and finally through the constituency parties to the ward and doorstep level. The parties have developed powerful bureaucracies and permanent staffs of their own – the Conservatives' Central Office and Labour's Transport House are across from each other in Smith Square in London. They run the national parties, the research, policy and other departments, and from these GHQs radiate highly organized links with regional, area and constituency organizations in a complete national network of political power. In the case of Labour there are the closest political ties between Transport House and the party's strongest allies, the trade unions; while the Conservatives' Central Office shares two main political links: the party chairmanship and professional full-time career structure of the party serving the central direction of the leadership, and the National Union (set up by Disraeli 100 years ago) which is the highly organized central power of the constituency and area bodies representing the party's grassroots.

The party machines are organized not only for waging the battles for political power but to support and serve the Parliamentary parties and, most of all, their leaderships.

Despite the whips and the party machines, it would be a serious mistake to underrate the importance and influence of backbench MPs. Admittedly the power of the party machines is overwhelming, able if need be to crush rebels to the point of annihilation, but MPs of character, ability and enterprise can influence Governments and policies to a notable degree. There have been several recent instances of backbench MPs compelling their Governments to abandon vital Bills. Perhaps the most notable example of what they can accomplish on their own is to be found in the field of social and personal reforms. A great many people know about A. P. Herbert's famous and successful one-man campaign to get divorce reform through; and in the past few years private bills introduced by private MPs have been responsible for effecting quite major and controversial reforms like the abolition of hanging and changes in the law for homosexuality, abortion, clean air, censorship of obscene publications, treatment of paraplegics and the permanently disabled. Parliament like any debating group can quickly assess the character and ability of its members, their strengths and their weaknesses; and such is the instinct and judgment of the Commons, irrespective of party, that the verdict invariably proves to be accurate. The most influential and respected MPs are not those who occupy most column inches in Hansard, because their colleagues' tests are much more subtle, accurate and revealing in assessing their true stature. As Nigel Nicolson wrote in *People and Parliament*, 'It is not only the antiquity of Parliament which cuts a man down to size. It is its terrible power to sum up character and detect fraud. Like a television camera, Parliament catches him at its weakest and most exposed'.

William Rees-Mogg, editor of *The Times* and himself a former Conservative candidate, wrote in a pamphlet after the 1964 General Election: 'The ordinary Member of Parliament is by-passed on every side. He is by-passed by the relationship between the Executive and television and the Press. Ministers will as a matter of course submit to questioning by lobby correspondents which they would not submit to in the House of Commons. They will answer questions on television which they have actually evaded or refused to answer in the House of Commons. This is matched by the relationship between the Executive and the big power groups in the country. The trade unions expect to deal direct with Government and regard the trade union Members of Parliament as a quite unimportant adjunct to their power. Business deals direct with the Government and does not even bother to seek representation in the House of Commons.'

Broadly the criticism is true, but inadequate attention is paid to the considerable influence deployed by the most powerful among backbench MPs, in direct and personal contact with their leaders and Ministers, and notably at the private meetings of their Parliamentary parties and party committees and area groups, where often conflicts over new policies and issues are more strenuously threshed out within parties than in the set debating pieces on the floor of the House.

Lord Campion wrote that a Member of Parliament 'like a delegate to the electoral college for the election of an American President, is returned primarily as a tied voter for a potential Prime Minister'. But perhaps Bagehot was more accurate when describing an MP as 'always a member of an assembly, never a Delegate from his constituency'.

CHAPTER 8

The life of an MP

At Westminster, Members of Parliament of all parties are kept at full stretch on a most exhausting and punishing treadmill. Most of them work a twelve to fourteen hour day, many of them much longer. Most Standing Committees on the committee stage of Bills of all kinds sit from 10.30 am to one o'clock two or three mornings every week (with afternoon and evening sittings as well on contentious and long drawn out measures), and this means an even earlier visit to collect their mail – for busy constituencies the daily tally of letters runs between fifty and a hundred.

Then the daily session in the Commons continues from 2.30 pm to 10.30 pm at the very minimum, though often it runs to midnight and even later. And during his day at Westminster the MP has to cope with many personal constituency cases; constituents arrive unexpectedly on most days and send in the 'green cards' which give the name of the MP, the constituent's name, and the business to be discussed. In many instances the Member has to entertain his visitors to tea, lunch or dinner as part of the endless calls on his hospitality. In addition, most days are fully occupied with meetings of specialist, party or area group meetings which he must attend – in addition to the debates in the actual chamber.

Then at the weekends he has to be in his constituency,

to attend social functions and his 'clinic' for his constituents, when he is available to talk privately with them about their personal, family and business problems which require follow up action by him in contact with Government Departments.

Increasingly Members are becoming welfare officers and pastoral advisers, giving comfort and counsel on how their constituents' worries and difficulties may be resolved; a massive problem in view of the extent to which State and Departmental policies and powers now affect the rights and interests of the individual and his family.

Inevitably Members live a mobile family life between their constituencies, a temporary flat in London often close to Westminster, and their private home where they hope to spend some time with their wives and children away from Westminster and the local constituency. But the opportunities to get away from the House are strictly limited, while Members who attempt to combine Parliamentary life with private and professional careers outside expose themselves to great physical strain, owing to the enormous pressure of the demands of professional politics.

Mr. Selwyn Lloyd, a respected elder statesman, former Foreign Secretary and Chancellor of the Exchequer, and now Mr. Speaker, wrote an interesting and revealing article in *The Reader's Digest*, May 1970 edition, on the theme that 'It's Time the Commons Put Their House in Order'. He argued that the House, overwhelmed by the sheer volume of its own work, is failing badly to keep pace with the demands of modern society. MPs are overworked, understaffed and badly accommodated in conditions reminiscent of the nineteenth century. He was surprised when he first became an MP that 'the basic equipment for my job consisted of a coat-hanger, a peg on which to hang a sword, and a locker for documents,

2 ft by 3 ft, that was smaller than the one I'd had at school'. Only 30 per cent of MPs – fewer than 200 – have rooms of their own; even fewer have a share of a room at the House itself. The rest are offered desks in buildings up to a quarter of a mile away. Secretaries are even worse, he adds; thirty share a room.

However, after a long experience of observing Westminster at first hand – almost daily for nearly forty years – the author is convinced that, despite the criticisms, the standard, quality and influence of Parliament has not really declined; indeed, the overall standard of MPs of all parties is incomparably higher today than at any time in that period. Critics have been complaining about the decline in the status and influence of Parliaments for 150 years at least, obsessed by their prophecies of the early collapse of the Parliamentary system itself. Their Jeremiads are even gloomier today, despite the notable increase in the educational quality of MPs and their all-round ability – though with politics becoming increasingly a younger man's game, each new intake appears to be less experienced in professional and business life than was the case, say, thirty years ago, when new MPs in most cases were in their late forties or early fifties, had first made their mark in careers outside, and had reached Westminster with established reputations.

The greatest need today is for the procedures, services and accommodation to be modernized, because the conditions under which MPs try to perform their demanding responsibilities as legislators are prehistoric compared with the facilities and services provided in Washington and in many Parliaments elsewhere.

Technically an MP cannot directly resign his Parliamentary seat, and where personal circumstances arise when he finds compelling reasons to leave the House he can only do so by applying for stewardship of 'The Chiltern Hundreds' or 'The Manor of Northstead'. This odd procedure is yet another example of how centuries-old traditions serve modern needs.

As a safeguard against abuse of patronage, it has long been Parliamentary law that if an MP accepts an 'office of profit under the Crown' (which means a State appointment with a State salary) he is automatically barred from continuing as MP. For several centuries the offices of steward or bailiff of Her Majesty's three Chiltern Hundreds of Stoke, Desborough and Burnham, and steward of the Manor of Northstead, have been nominal offices of profit. They simply do not exist today, and are just a convenient myth, but they provide a traditional and handy means of enabling an MP to retire from Parliament; the formula provides that the Member must be appointed to the Chiltern Hundreds by the Chancellor of the Exchequer.

Another case of mumbo-jumbo? Perhaps, but at least it enables the resignation of an MP to be effected neatly, simply and without fuss, by making use of obsolete offices to serve modern needs. It also recognizes that MPs must have convincing grounds for resigning from Parliament, not acting merely to meet their own convenience.

CHAPTER 9

The purpose of Opposition

The Opposition, in its theory and practice, was invented and perfected in Britain, and today is one of the basic features in the smooth working of the entire Parliamentary system. It is a hardy well-established British plant though it has not travelled well, except in the old white Commonwealth countries, where its growth still flourishes. An effective and powerful Opposition is an essential pre-condition for good Government and a democratic Parliament.

At Westminster you will notice that, under the rules of procedure, the Opposition is given parity of treatment and recognition to that of the Government itself; the Opposition has a built-in status of its own in the daily working of the constitution.

The Prime Minister and his senior Cabinet colleagues occupy the front Treasury bench on the Speaker's right; immediately opposite them are the Leader of the Opposition and his Shadow Cabinet.

The description 'His Majesty's Opposition' was first coined by Lord Broughton in 1828 in a derisory sense, and was at once welcomed by Canning, who said that a better phrase could not have been invented: 'for we are certainly to all intents and purposes a branch of His Majesty's Government. Its proceedings for some time past have proved that though the gentlemen opposite are in office, we are in power. The measures are ours, but the emoluments are theirs.'

Britain, as it were, patented the whole concept of Opposition specially to criticize, question and, if possible, defeat the Government of the day. The official descriptions give the clue: against 'Her Majesty's Government' we have 'Her Majesty's Opposition' a balance which recognizes that the role of criticizing and opposing the Government is just as much part of the working of the democratic system as is the job of the Government in governing.

So therefore it is not anomalous that the Leader of the Opposition is paid a salary of £9,500 by the State, and the Opposition Chief Whip £7,500 in order to maintain efficient Opposition, and if possible, overthrow the Government and take its place at the first opportunity. The Government, through the Treasury, provides salaries to its principal opponents and critics, who have a vested interest in exposing the shortcomings of the sitting Prime Minister and his Cabinet.

The job of Opposition Leader is lonely and responsible. As Disraeli said: 'There are few positions less inspiriting than that of the leader of a discomfited party. He who in the Parliamentary field watches over the fortunes of routed troops must be prepared often to sit alone. Few care to share the labour which is doomed to be fruitless, and none are eager to diminish the responsibility of him whose course, however adroit, must necessarily be ineffectual'.

The Opposition leader who may be called upon to form a new Government as the alternative Prime Minister, creates more than a Shadow Cabinet; he also appoints the complex duplication of a Government down to the most junior of shadow spokesmen.

Opposition, however, has not been one of our most

successful exports. The Westminster model of Government and Parliament has been established in a few dozen emerging and newly independent countries, advancing from former Colonial rule to their own national identities, but the theory of Opposition has not taken root; all too often the new constitutions have reverted to one-party rule, intolerant of an organized alternative waiting to take over. Oppositions in emerging countries have frequently been crushed by the simple expedient of declaring them illegal.

In Britain the practice of Opposition lies at the very heart of our two-party system. The presence of a vigorous, persistent and confident Opposition is a constant reminder and warning to the Government that it may be thrown out at the next General Election, while the Opposition is sustained by the hope and ambition to be seen as the ready-made alternative, the Government-in-waiting.

The system works best when there is a mutual understanding between the two front benches, however deeply they disagree in their political convictions, concerning what life in this country is about. There are indeed constant, often daily, contacts and consultations between them on a personal, behind-the-scenes basis which could never happen without this national harmony. These take the form of discussions on business, priorities of debate and the arrangement of the Parliamentary timetable or agenda between the two Chief Whips and their teams: these talks take place through the usual channels, the euphemism to describe the confidential aspect of exchanges on business.

The Opposition, too, has the right to select subjects for debate on its own initiative on thirty-two days during a session; and as an Opposition does not exist to make life easy and comfortable for a Government, the debates they request are invariably on policies and events calculated to cause the maximum embarrassment to the Government. In an average session the Opposition controls about a third of the sitting days when it has freedom to select the subjects for debate and inquiry.

When the Prime Minister opens a major debate with an important speech he is usually followed by the Opposition leader, and for the remainder of the time the Speaker keeps a fair balance between the parties (and frequently within the parties as well when there are domestic disagreements) by calling Government and Opposition speakers alternately. The Opposition has also a reserve challenge at its disposal, by its right to table censure or no confidence motions when it feels that the Government, or even an individual Minister, has been culpable of inefficiency or responsible for some injustice. Such censure motions are debated without delay when they are tabled officially by the Opposition leader and members of his Shadow Cabinet – another reminder of the status given to the Opposition, which can become the new Government by the marginal swing of public opinion.

Thus it is the role of the Opposition to build itself up as the responsible and acceptable alternative Administration ready to move in whenever the country calls. To this end, day after day, on big issues and on trivial ones, the Opposition must keep the Government under scrutiny and pressure, forever questioning Ministers and keeping them fully stretched.

One-party dictatorships do not encourage alternative parties. In Britain, the presence of a vigorous and responsible Opposition makes a vital contribution to the political health of the country. A fairly long experience of many Governments and Oppositions convinces the author that a well-led and strong Opposition has always had the most salutary effect upon improving the health and efficiency of the Government; only weak Oppositions allow weak Governments to survive.

In the case of the late Hugh Gaitskell, it is widely recognized that his leadership of the Labour Party in Opposition had as profound an impact upon events and the history of the period as members of the Cabinet. That gives you the measure of the importance of a vigorous Opposition in maintaining the highest standards of political life.

Over a wide range of Parliamentary affairs, the Opposition has freedom to exploit its own initiative. While it is true that in the vast majority of issues the Government can dictate the pace and direction of events, a vigorous and well-led Opposition can play a notable role by focusing and projecting attention on subjects which the Cabinet might prefer to ignore or forget. The Prime Minister sees the leader of the Opposition as the menacing alternative to himself, the heir presumptive eager to seize the throne. To the visitor the battle between them may seem an artificial Tweedledum and Tweedledee contest, but the confrontation between them is no charade; power is what politics is all about, for without power, ideals and policies can never be realised.

A long spell in Opposition can prove a dispiriting experience, and clearly the biggest challenge facing an Opposition leader, who lacks power, office and patronage, is to sustain a high morale among his troops. If he is ever to form a Government of his own he must present himself and his party as the responsible, acceptable and well-prepared alternative, establishing an impressive reputation for public and national service, championing causes, policies, ideals and campaigns which strike a sympathetic chord with public opinion. Some say that Oppositions never win elections, only that Governments lose them, but this theory does not tell the full story, and ignores the fact that the best Oppositions can exercise a profound in-uence on national and world events, equal almost to that of the best Governments.

CHAPTER 10

General Election rules

The Parliament Act of 1911 fixes the maximum lifetime of Parliament at five years, though usually Prime Ministers, who have the sole prerogative and responsibility of deciding when to go to the country, prefer to hold general elections after three-and-a-half to four-and-a-half years in office, judging the timing when they consider it suits them and their party's interest. There have been occasions, admittedly very rare, when Parliaments have run their full five years; and in the two World Wars, when Coalition governments were in power, legislation was passed exempting the wartime Parliaments from the limits of the quinquennial system until peace returned. In theory, when a Government is defeated in the House of Commons on a major issue involving confidence in the Administration, a General Election follows at once, but under the rigidity of the modern party system such defeats are very exceptional, although there are a few precedents where elections took place at the end of Coalition governments, as the result of one of the parties withdrawing support and leaving a vulnerable minority Government on its own without any real chance of surviving.

A General Election is announced when the Queen, acting on the advice of her Prime Minister, brings Parliament to an end by the Royal Prerogative of Dissolution and at the same time, by Royal Proclamation, summons the next Parliament to meet in its place on a specified date after the General Election. On an average about five weeks' advance notice is given of polling day; monination of candidates is submitted to the Returning Officers (usually the local Sheriffs or Mayors) in each of the 630 constituencies eight days after the dissolution of the old Parliament, with polling day (always a Thursday in modern times) on the twenty-first day of the campaign. Candidates are required to make a deposit of £150, which is forfeited if they fail to poll at least one-eighth of the total votes cast in the constituency.

British citizens are eligible to become candidates with the following exceptions: minors under twenty-one (despite the fact that the voting age was reduced to eighteen in time for the 1970 election), lunatics, bankrupts, traitors or felons serving imprisonment, peers (except Irish peers), clergymen of the Roman Catholic or the established Churches, judges, civil servants on the active list. Unlike the American system, candidates need not live in their constituencies, though many of them do when they become Members of Parliament.

The duration of a Parliament is normally sub-divided into sessions, which usually last for one year each, from November to November, opened by the Queen's Speech which announces the Government's programme for the next twelve months. In the normal run of events, barring major emergencies, Parliament sits for about nine months every year, broken by recesses for Christmas, Easter, Whitsun, and the longer autumn holiday.

The main objective of the General Election is not only to enable each constituency to elect a Member of its own choice, important though that is, but by an aggregation of constituencies to enable the country to choose the nature and party colour of the Government it wants to be returned to power. Members are elected by simple majority; this country has never been favourably disposed to proportional representation, the alternative transferable vote, and other more complicated systems.

As noted in chapter 7, independent candidates who oppose the established parties have the most negligible prospects of attracting a substantial share of the votes, let alone of ever being elected. While the theory of electoral law presupposes that anyone may be elected a Member of Parliament, the reality is that only candidates of the main parties are elected: which means that an MP is nominated and elected on the party ticket and is thus broadly committed to toe the party line (a system which makes doubly certain that rebels have seldom a long-term chance of surviving once they break company from the party machine).

CHAPTER II

How Laws are made

Ask almost anyone what is the main function of Parliament and he will say that it is to pass laws. This impression is widespread, but it is only partially accurate. In an average session only about sixty per cent of the Parliamentary time is occupied with debates on legislation – proposed new laws are set out in Bills when they are introduced in Parliament and become Acts when they are passed through both Houses and finally receive the Royal Assent.

In tracing the progress of Bills from a basic idea to the final achievement of Royal Assent when they are added to the statute book, we shall deal first with official Government Bills, which comprise about ninety per cent of the new legislation and represent the Administration's policies and legislative programmes; in addition, as already mentioned, there are Bills introduced by private Members of Parliament in their personal capacity. (There is yet another category of private Bills promoted by local authorities, public corporations and public utilities, but these are highly specialized, and go through technical procedures of their own which do not impinge upon the daily business at Westminster).

All parties fight General Elections on policy programmes outlined in their manifestoes, so that every incoming Government is committed in advance to a considerable number of Bills. In addition, all Departments in Whitehall have their own favourite measures in their pending trays which the officials hope will be adopted by their Ministers, after due persuasion, and submitted to the Cabinet for inclusion in the Government's programme announced in the Queen's Speech. Every Government finds without fail that there are always far more deserving and prospective Bills in the queue than can possibly be fitted in; in resolving this dilemma it is not a question of deciding which Bills are really desirable and necessary but which really desirable and necessary Bills can be passed in the relatively short time available.

There is always great rivalry and competition among Cabinet Ministers to get their Bills included in the Queen's Speech, and well placed at the start for a quick getaway, because to be in charge of major measures, which are often highly controversial and inevitably occupy the centre of the Parliamentary stage for a long period and attract the public limelight, brings welcome opportunity for building up personal and political prestige as well as Parliamentary status and reputation.

This is how the procedure works. Ministers submit their proposals and departmental recommendations to the Cabinet Legislation Committee, usually chaired by the Lord President of the Council when he is Leader of the House of Commons as well. The Government Chief Whip has often a vital role to play in the early studies of the suggested Bill. With his knowledge of the state of opinion inside the party he can restrain the excessive enthusiasm of Ministers by warning them that his 'chaps won't stand for it' – and there is nothing more worrying for Ministers than the threat of a party revolt against them. Similarly, the Chief Whip can stiffen Ministers' courage to proceed with a contentious Bill by the counsel

Notice how policies develop from the initial idea to the final legislative enactment. In this case the sequence starts with the Conservative Party Manifesto at the General Election in 1970 ... Note that on page 12 of the Manifesto (opposite), the Party is committed to legislate on reforming Industrial Relations ...

that if it is not introduced to honour an election pledge 'I'll not be able to hold the party – MPs are demanding action by the Government and won't accept excuses'.

When Cabinet approval is given to the introduction of a particular Bill in the Government's programme, the files are passed to the Parliamentary Council, the team of experts whose special task it is to prepare the Bill line by line and clause by clause: a very complex operation, because new Bills have to be interpreted by lawyers, judged by the courts, put into effect by administrators, and respected by the mass of citizens.

The Parliamentary Counsel and his small staff of lawyers, who have become civil servants in a branch of the Treasury, frequently prepare a dozen to a score of drafts of a Bill, passing all the time between Departments who, fighting their own corner, submit amendments and proposals before the final version is approved and ready for presentation to Parliament.

subject all proposed price rises in the public sector to the most searching scrutiny. If they are not justified, they will not be allowed. In implementing our policies, we will give overriding priority to bringing the present inflation under control.

Fair Deal at Work

There were more strikes in 1969 than ever before in our history. Already in the first three months of 1970 there were 1,134 strikes compared with 718 in the same period last year, when the Labour Government said the position was so serious that legislation was essential in the national interest. This rapid and serious deterioration directly stems from Labour's failure to carry through its own policy for the reform of industrial relations.

We will introduce a comprehensive Industrial Relations Bill in the first Session of the new Parliament. It will provide a proper framework of law within which improved relationships between management, men and unions can develop. We welcome the TUC's willingness to take action through its own machinery against those who disrupt industrial peace by unconstitutional or unofficial action. Yet it is no substitute for the new set of fair and reasonable rules we will introduce.

We aim to strengthen the unions and their official leadership by providing some deterrent against irresponsible action by unofficial minorities. We seek to create conditions in which strikes become the means of last resort, not of first resort, as they now so often are.

Our new Act will establish clear rights and obligations for unions and employers. It will lay down what is lawful and what is not lawful in the conduct of industrial disputes. It will also introduce new safeguards for the individual—the right of appeal against unjust dismissal by an employer or unjust action by a union.

The framework of law we will establish will provide for agreements to be binding on both unions and employers. A new Registrar of Trades Unions and Employers' Associations will ensure that their rules are fair, just, democratic, and not in conflict with the public interest. In the case of a dispute which would seriously endanger the national interest, our Act will provide for the holding of a secret ballot and for a 'cooling-off period' of not less than sixty days.

Associated with our new Act will be a Code of Practice laying down guidelines for good collective agreements and standards for good management and trade union practices in the individual company.

Every Bill opens with this preamble:

> 'Be it enacted by the Queen's most Excellent Majesty, by and with the advice and consent of the Lords Spiritual and Temporal, and Commons in this Parliament assembled, and by the authority of the same, as follows'.

Then follow the detailed provisions of the Bill, now ready for its Parliamentary premiere. On the day selected, the Order Paper, under the heading of 'At the commencement of public business' will carry for the first time the long title and short title of the Bill, with the name of the Minister introducing it. When the entry is called the Minister bows in acknowledgement, the short title is read out, and at the request of the Speaker – 'Which day?' – the Minister names the date for second reading.

The Bill once launched on its Parliamentary journey, goes through identical stages in both Lords and Commons:

First Reading;
Second Reading;
Committee Stage;
Report Stage;
Third Reading; and finally the
Royal Assent signified by Royal Commission.

Why *third* readings then, after so much has gone before? The reason is that the number three was always treated with mystical respect in medieval times and became a feature of reverence in early Parliamentary procedures. In more practical terms, third readings provide the final chance for the final judgment to be spoken, disposing of the risk of any ill-judged legislation being rushed through without adequate consideration.

The word 'read' is misleading. The Bills are not in

fact 'read' at their First, Second and Third Readings, which are really euphemisms for their presentation, study and debate – clearly to 'read' a massive Bill of hundreds of pages, containing as many clauses and sections would occupy enormous time without any left over for debate.

The First Reading is only a formality. The Clerk reads out the Short Title of the Bill, which is only formally presented, and authority is given for its printing by the Stationery Office. That is all the First Reading is about: a Bill has been born and next day it is available in detail for distribution to MPs, Press and the public, including interested outside bodies most likely to be affected.

Usually about two or three weeks later comes the Second Reading. This is the occasion for the first big debate on the Bill's principles and objectives rather than its precise details. On the day fixed the Speaker announces 'The question is that the Bill be now read a second time', and calls on Mr. So-and-so, who is the Minister responsible for the measure, to move the motion for its approval in a major policy speech devoted to its merits. Then the Opposition Shadow Minister follows with a speech analyzing or criticizing the Bill, depending on whether his party approves of it in general, but wants to amend and improve it in Committee, or violently disagrees with its whole purpose leading to outright opposition at every stage. After the two opening speeches, the debate is thrown open to backbenchers until about nine o'clock in the evening, when the winding up speech is delivered for the Opposition, then the final word for the last half-hour by the Minister's Under-Secretary or, if the occasion is an important one involving confidence, by a Cabinet or senior colleague.

At ten o'clock, the Speaker puts the motion for the Second Reading, the Government's supporters shout

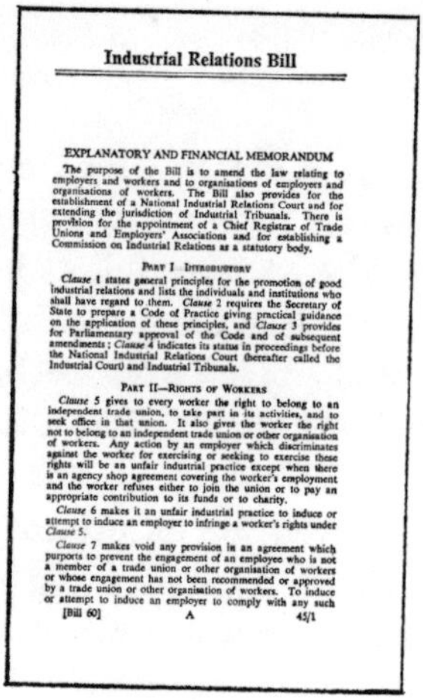

Industrial Relations Bill

EXPLANATORY AND FINANCIAL MEMORANDUM

The purpose of the Bill is to amend the law relating to employers and workers and to organisations of employers and organisations of workers. The Bill also provides for the establishment of a National Industrial Relations Court and for extending the jurisdiction of Industrial Tribunals. There is provision for the appointment of a Chief Registrar of Trade Unions and Employers' Associations and for establishing a Commission on Industrial Relations as a statutory body.

PART I INTRODUCTORY

Clause 1 states general principles for the promotion of good industrial relations and lists the individuals and institutions who shall have regard to them. *Clause* 2 requires the Secretary of State to prepare a Code of Practice giving practical guidance on the application of these principles, and *Clause* 3 provides for Parliamentary approval of the Code and of subsequent amendments; *Clause* 4 indicates its status in proceedings before the National Industrial Relations Court (hereafter called the Industrial Court) and Industrial Tribunals.

PART II—RIGHTS OF WORKERS

Clause 5 gives to every worker the right to belong to an independent trade union, to take part in its activities, and to seek office in that union. It also gives the worker the right not to belong to an independent trade union or other organisation of workers. Any action by an employer which discriminates against the worker for exercising or seeking to exercise these rights will be an unfair industrial practice except when there is an agency shop agreement covering the worker's employment and the worker refuses either to join the union or to pay an appropriate contribution to its funds or to charity.

Clause 6 makes it an unfair industrial practice to induce or attempt to induce an employer to infringe a worker's rights under *Clause* 5.

Clause 7 makes void any provision in an agreement which purports to prevent the engagement of an employee who is not a member of a trade union or other organisation of workers or whose engagement has not been recommended or approved by a trade union or other organisation of workers. To induce or attempt to induce an employer to comply with any such

[Bill 60] A 45/1

Page 1 of the controversial Bill, of formidable size, comprising 150 clauses, 8 schedules, and 138 pages. After a contentious Committee stage, strenuously fought on both sides, with prolonged and often angry all-night sittings, the Bill finally became an Act, when it received the Royal Assent and reached the Statute Book six months later.

'Aye', the Opposition MPs to the contrary bellow 'No'; the Speaker prepares for the detailed vote by demanding 'Clear the Lobbies', 'Ayes to the Right, Noes to the Left, tellers for the Ayes Mr. So-and-so and Mr. Blankety-Blank, tellers for the Noes Mr. Dogsbody and Mr. Such-and-Such.' The tellers are usually two party Whips on each side. The bells start ringing all over the building, even in those clubs and private homes close by specially wired for the purpose, to enable MPs to make a dash for it in the six to nine minutes available before the division lobbies (which run parallel to the chamber on each side) are shut at the command of the Speaker: 'Lock the doors'. Heads are counted by the tellers representing both sides as MPs pass through the exit doors, their names ticked off on the alphabetical division lists by official clerks. At the close the tellers return to the Chamber and report to the Speaker: 'Ayes to the Right ... 299; Noes to the Left ... 201.' And thereupon Mr. Speaker declares the Second Reading carried.

In the details of the legislative plans of the new Government, announced in the Queen's Speech (opposite), there is the promise to bring in a Bill to reform the law of industrial relations affecting the trade unions.

Members of the House of Commons

Estimates for the public services will be laid before you.

My Lords and Members of the House of Commons

At home My Government's first concern will be to strengthen the economy and curb the inflation. Rising production and a steadily growing national income must provide the resources for improving the social services and the environment in which we live. The energy and enterprise needed to achieve this will be encouraged by reforming and reducing the burden of taxation, providing new incentives to saving and liberating industry from unnecessary intervention by Government.

My Ministers attach the greatest importance to promoting full employment and an effective regional development policy. They will stimulate long-term growth in the less prosperous areas by increasing their economic attractions and improving their amenities.

My Ministers will start discussions with a view to encouraging agricultural expansion by changes in the present system of financial support. They will promote the efficient development of the fishing industry.

The work of the Industrial Training Boards will be reviewed and the facilities for re-training and for management training improved and extended.

A Bill will be introduced to establish a framework of law within which improved industrial relations can develop and a code of practice will be prepared laying down standards for good management and trade union practice.

My Government believe that vigorous competition is the best safeguard for the consumer. They will carry out a review of company law.

My Ministers will pursue a vigorous housing policy with the principal aim of improving the position of the homeless and the badly housed. After consultations with local authorities, housing subsidies will be refashioned so as to give more help to those in greatest need. Home ownership will be encouraged.

My Government will expand educational opportunities as growing resources make this possible, with priority for the improvement of primary schools. An inquiry will be instituted into teacher training. Local authorities in Scotland, as in England and Wales, will be set free to take effective decisions on the organisation of their schools.

Responsibility for primary and secondary education in Wales will be assumed by the Secretary of State for Wales.

Legislation will be brought forward to provide pensions for persons now over 80 who were too old to enter the present insurance scheme and for certain younger widows and to provide a constant attendance allowance for the very seriously disabled.

Legislation will be introduced on Commonwealth immigration. More assistance will be provided for areas of special social need, especially those in which large numbers of immigrants have settled.

The voting procedures have proved very accurate throughout the centuries, although there is the story in Parliamentary lore suggesting that the famous Habeas Corpus Act of 1679, central to our liberties, was only passed by accident, thanks to a teller facetiously counting a fat lord as ten lords. Burnet in *History of his own Time* recounts the event: 'Lord Grey and Lord Norris were named to be tellers. Lord Norris being a man subject to vapours, was not at all times attentive to what he was doing; so a very fat lord coming in, Lord Grey counted him for ten, as a jest at first, but seeing Lord Norris had not observed it, he went on with this misreckoning of ten; so it was reported to the House and declared that they who were for the Bill were the majority, though indeed it went on the other side; and by this means the Bill passed'.

The Second Reading hurdle safely over, the Bill comes to its Committee stage. This is really its toughest and most exhausting test. Very important measures involving major policy are put before a 'Committee of the whole House', which means that it is sent to the entire Commons sitting in Committee. The main distinction is that the Speaker does not preside, but the Chairman of Committees as Deputy Speaker takes over. There is some argument among historians when the rule for the Speaker to withdraw during the Committee stage was first introduced, but it is most widely agreed that it was probably introduced at the time of James I to make certain that Mr. Speaker, usually a nominee of the Crown in those days, was not in the chair during debates on important details.

In the vast majority of cases, however, the Bill is sent to a Standing committee 'upstairs' (it sits in one of the series of Committee Rooms in the upper corridor where the Committee rooms are laid out as miniature Commons chambers). Each Standing Committee usually consists of between thirty and fifty MPs, with the Members on the Government and Opposition sides proportionate in numbers to the overall strength of the parties in the Commons. This can be a tight squeeze, with a Committee's paper majority of only one or two when the Government of the day only has the narrowest of margins in the Commons; on big Bills hundreds of amendments are tabled with the varied purpose of improving, moderating, or even wrecking the most contentious clauses.

If the Bill is making very slow progress, due to obstruction by its critics, its passage can be speeded up by the adoption of either the 'guillotine' or 'kangaroo' system. The guillotine imposes time-limits for groups of clauses and amendments, which must be dealt with in the allotted time, even if it excludes debate on some important clauses because MPs have spent (or wasted) too much time on earlier ones. The kangaroo, on the other hand, empowers the Chairman to select amendments, ignore others, or decide that several should be taken simultaneously.

Inevitably, when these devices are used, especially the guillotine, the Government of the day is always accused of gagging its opponents and steamrollering all arguments. But for most hotly contested and controversial Bills, it is the only way of ever getting them through Committee. A third device for shortening prolonged debate and excessive opposition is to apply the closure, which takes the form of the Whip in charge moving that 'The question be now put', in order to put an end to long-running argument by the critics. But even the closure procedure is laborious; on big occasions most Governments opt decisively for the guillotine to see them through.

The Committee stage safely over, our Bill is then sent

Then, six months after the Election, comes the outline of the Government's proposals, in this case in the form of a Consultative Document to stimulate public discussion.

INDUSTRIAL RELATIONS BILL : CONSULTATIVE DOCUMENT

Contents

INDUSTRIAL RELATIONS BILL : CONSULTATIVE DOCUMENT

I: INTRODUCTION

1. The Government has made clear its intention to introduce a comprehensive Industrial Relations Bill during the present session of Parliament.

2. This document sets out the principles on which the Government proposes that the Bill should be based, and the main provisions which it proposes to include. It is intended to serve as a basis for consultations with the Trades Union Congress and the Confederation of British Industry; the Government wishes to start these consultations without delay. The Government will also welcome comments from other interested organisations and individuals. Details of where to send these comments, and of how to obtain further copies of the document, will be found at the end.

3. The improvement of industrial relations is of great importance both from an economic and from a social point of view. Poor industrial relations adversely affect output, raise industrial costs, damage the balance of payments, and inhibit industrial investment. They also restrict people's opportunities of finding satisfaction in their work, and create avoidable conflicts and hostilities in the workplace and in society as a whole. They dissipate the energies of management and unions alike, which are needed for more constructive purposes.

4. Poor industrial relations are not to be equated simply with strikes. They include many other kinds of failure in human relations in employment. The remedies are primarily the responsibility of management, in whose hands rests the initiative for any improvements that the circumstances may permit.

5. Strikes are, however, often an important sympton of poor industrial relations. And they can make poor industrial relations still worse, particularly when agreed procedures for resolving disputes are ignored, or when one group's pursuit of its sectional interests leads to conflict with other employees. Unions and employees have a responsibility, as well as management, to see that their actions are directed towards securing and maintaining good industrial relations.

6. Whatever changes are made, the present widespread shortcomings of industrial relations in Britain cannot be expected to disappear overnight. But they will not disappear at all unless managements, and the representatives of employees, intensify their efforts to identify and resolve the problems that arise between managements and employees. The improvement and strengthening of machinery for negotiation and consultation, for example, is crucial. Where such efforts have been forthcoming, substantial improvements in industrial relations have been secured.

7. For its part, the Government will continue to encourage progress towards better industrial relations by the example it sets as an employer and by the help and encouragement it can give through its specialist services which provide advice and conciliate in disputes.

8. But more is required. Government has a responsibility to make clear the standards to which, on behalf of the country as a whole, it expects the conduct of industrial relations to conform, to establish safeguards for the individual and the community, and to provide the means for resolving disputes over the machinery of industrial relations and the behaviour of the parties to it. The proposed Industrial Relations Act will be the Government's main instrument in achieving these objectives.

9. The Government therefore sees the proposals set out for comment in this document as complementary, and essential, to a continuing and

back to the whole House, first for its Report Stage and then its Third Reading. The Report stage is really the final chance for the House to consider the details and further amendments, but these must not go over ground well covered in Committee. In practice, Report enables the Government to introduce changes promised earlier in Committee or to meet cases where the Minister in charge had undertaken to consider in greater detail some particular amendment to see what he could do to meet a genuine problem or anomaly.

After the Report procedure, which is seldom lively or interesting, comes the Third Reading; which is really a repetition of the Second Reading debate on general principles and aims, but with the chance to add the final word on any changes which had been made in Committee.

The Bill, its Commons journey completed, is now sent to the House of Lords where it goes through broadly the identical stages and procedures, though here amendments, in certain circumstances, can be moved (and carried) at the Third Reading Stage. If the Lords amend the Bill it is then sent back to the Commons for an additional procedure: 'on consideration of the Lords' amendments'. If these amendments improve the wording and structure of the measure the Commons welcome and approve their lordships' handiwork: 'That this House doth agree with the Lords in the said amendment'. But in instances of sharp disagreement it is a case of, after brief debate, 'That this House doth disagree with the Lords in the said amendment' and the Bill, with the Lords' amendments struck out, is returned to the Upper House which almost always accedes to the Commons verdict at the second time round.

Our Bill now awaits the Royal Assent. Not since Queen Victoria's time has the Sovereign been present in person

Industrial Relations

A

BILL

TO

Amend the law relating to employers and workers and to organisations of employers and organisations of workers; to provide for the establishment of a National Industrial Relations Court and for extending the jurisdiction of industrial tribunals; to provide for the appointment of a Chief Registrar of Trade Unions and Employers' Associations, and of assistant registrars, and for establishing a Commission on Industrial Relations as a statutory body; and for purposes connected with those matters.

Presented by Mr. Secretary Carr,
supported by
The Prime Minister, Mr. Secretary Maudling,
Mr. Chancellor of the Exchequer,
Mr. William Whitelaw,
Secretary Sir Keith Joseph,
Mr. Secretary Davies, Mr. Secretary Campbell,
Mr. Solicitor General and Mr. Dudley Smith

Ordered, by The House of Commons,
to be Printed, 1 *December* 1970

LONDON
Printed and Published by
Her Majesty's Stationery Office
Printed in England at St. Stephen's
Parliamentary Press

18s. 0d. [90p] net

[Bill 60] (378127) 45/1

The great moment arrives, the Industrial Relations Bill is introduced in Parliament ... above the short title, with the sponsors named.

to promulgate final approval. The established procedure is for a Royal Commission appointed under the Great Seal to announce the Crown's approval in Norman French, 'la Reine le veult' in a 600-year old ceremonial, with the Commissioners in robes and little cocked hats seated immediately in front of the Throne in the House of Lords and in the presence of Mr. Speaker, ministers and MPs who are summoned from 'the faithful Commons' by messenger Black Rod to hear the Assent intoned. Not since the reign of Queen Anne has the royal rejection procedure been invoked 'la Reine s'avisera'.

We have dealt with the progress of official Government Bills, which are draft Acts of Parliament, on their way to the statute. In addition, there are a great many Bills introduced by backbench MPs either as a result of being drawn in a good position at or near the top of the Members' ballot for private legislation or under the Ten Minute Rule procedure (which does mean what it says, that the Bill can be introduced in ten minutes in the Commons, the maximum time permissible for speeches by the sponsor and the chief opponent). These Bills, which are introduced by backbench MPs, go through the same stages as Government Bills, the only difference being that the Members concerned, and not Ministers, are responsible for piloting the legislation. It frequently happens that the Government expresses its opinion of the privately presented Bills, which, where this is favourable, gives them a fair wind in facilitating their progress.

CHAPTER 12

Press, Radio and Television

It is not natural, not rational, that the people who sent us hither should not be informed of our actions.

Sir Francis Winnington, MP, 1681.

Parliament has always been shy of publicity and public relations, and today it is just as suspicious of the modern media of mass communications like television and radio as it was centuries ago over the first efforts at reporting debates for news-letters and news sheets. Then reporters were persecuted and prosecuted as strangers intruding upon secret proceedings. Even now radio microphones and TV cameras are banned as being of dubious value. In the old days newspapermen were sent to prison in the Clock Tower beside Big Ben for trying to establish the freedom of the Press and attempting to inform the people what MPs were doing in their name; today the television communicators are unlikely to be sent to prison, but they are nevertheless banned from recording the proceedings.

It is probable that in the end the public will receive some live broadcasts, in sound and picture, of the debates in both Houses – in this field the House of Lords has been ahead of the commons in pioneering experiments – especially of the great historic occasions. Television broadcasts in colour of the State Opening of Parliament by the Queen in the presence of the robed nobles and the bejewelled peeresses in glittering tiaras, make admirable viewing as was proved in 1970.

It was only in 1971 that Parliament finally conceded the right of the Press to report its proceedings, by finally rescinding the 1738 resolution, which decreed:

> [It is] a high indignity to and a notorious breach of privilege of this House for any newswriter in letters or other papers . . . to insert in the said letters or papers or to give therein any account of the debates or other proceedings of this House or any Committee thereof . . .; and that this House will proceed with the utmost severity against such offenders'.

There is no doubt about the 'utmost severity' with which the early reporters were pursued, even long before the resolution which has just been quoted. During the period from about 1560 to 1641, MPs, as though in a secret society, were compelled to keep 'secret things done and spoken in the Parliament House', and inevitably this drove contemporary writers and diarists underground. (After 1641 official records or minutes were kept, but only in the briefest form). The earliest offenders were called to the bar of the Commons, compelled to kneel and seek forgiveness, before being reprimanded; others were despatched to the Big Ben Tower prison for their defiance. The enterprising printers and reporters were championed by John Wilkes, the great impresario of civil liberty, and his campaign finally succeeded, when the House committed the Mayor and Aldermen of the City to prison for harbouring offenders like Wilkes. This provoked such widespread reactions that Parliament's insistence on secrecy collapsed, though the technical ban on reporting debates was kept on the records for another 250 years – just in case!

From then onwards the House gave up the struggle and

writers were admitted to mix with MPs in the lobbies and occupy seats in the galleries; Dr. Johnson was one of the early reporters, though his independence and accuracy could be qualified by his determination to ensure that the 'Whig dogs never got the best of it'. The recognition of the Press as 'The Fourth Estate' (Macaulay's phrase; there were three estates in Parliament, Monarch, Lords and Commons, while in the Reporters' Gallery sat, as he claimed, 'a fourth estate more important than them') all, dates from the early 1830s, when the first press gallery was built. The official verbatim record of proceedings started in 1803, and is still known as Hansard, after its first printer. A century ago the political and lobby correspondents established their right to be admitted to the Members' lobby to lobby Ministers and MPs.

There are now two main groups of journalists working in Parliament; the Parliamentary correspnodents who are primarily concerned with what actually takes place on the floor of the Chamber – debates, questions, scenes and the big events in the House; and the political and lobby correspondents who are concerned with policies, politics, political trends, and events behind the scenes in Government, Opposition and in all the parties and with personal liaison with Ministers and MPs. The daily attendance is close on 300, of whom about seventy are lobby correspondents (in addition, there is a special press gallery for commonwealth and foreign correspondents). There are also some twenty TV and radio journalists, but without their microphones and cameras. The networks have studios in nearby buildings.

The authorities of both parties appear as unwilling to allow reporting by radio and TV as they once were by the Press. Several debates, inquiries and closed circuit tests have taken place, but still the ban remains, the more surprising because TV and radio could make the more immediate impact by instant reports of events and decisions at Westminster. By one vote the Commons refused in 1966 to accept recommendations of a Select Committee for the proceedings of the House to be broadcast experimentally on a closed circuit; renewed efforts since have failed to alter this situation. The main proposal is worth recalling: 'Your Committee consider that the House would be wise to agree that its proceedings should be recorded for broadcasting, and that the people should thus be allowed to see and hear their representatives at work, unless it can be shown that to allow cameras and microphones into the Chamber would change the procedure, the character and the atmosphere of the House perceptibly for the worse'.

Continuous TV reporting of long day-to-day debates in Parliament would prove incredibly tedious, but there is a case for edited TV and sound reports of important debates and speeches, notably historic occasions. Ronald Butt summarized the arguments in his impressive book *The Power of Parliament*. TV cameras would 'help to restore the public's allegedly waning faith and interest in Parliamentary processes and would enable the electorate to see the battles of contemporary politics fought out in their proper arena and not simply re-staged in the artificial setting of television studios'.

There are obviously technical problems to be overcome before a satisfactory formula can be devised. As Maurice Edelman MP, put it in his evidence to the Select Committee inquiry in 1966: 'It seems to me that pictorial editing lends itself much more to caricature than verbal editing, because at least with words you are dealing with ideas whereas with pictures you are dealing with all sorts of aspects of the person photographed which are beyond his control'.

On this choice Ronald Butt comments that TV broadcasts would stress the personality aspects, rather than the issues of politics. 'If they are faced with a choice between an entertaining "personalities" episode or a painstaking account of, say, two worthy but unexciting front bench speeches which set out the arguments, television editors will be liable to use much of their space for the more entertaining and more easily presentable episode.' One hopes that Parliament in the end will come round to allowing the TV cameras and radio microphones to report the proceedings. It was not until 1862, after the fire of 1834, that a special press gallery was provided in the new Commons, designed by Sir Charles Barry, for the London newspapers, and in 1881, the provincial papers were admitted. To this day, Press photographers are not allowed in the House. Only on a few occasions in this century have photographs been taken in the Chamber of the House of Commons, the first time being in 1950, when the rebuilt Commons was officially opened. Penalties await a correspondent who wants to use a silent tape to help in his reporting work!

The main objection to TV colour cameras being allowed to report Parliamentary debates is that their presence would inevitably encourage a new generation of extroverts, showmen and performer MPs, even a new frightening race of political entrepreneurs anxious to improve their 'pop' ratings with their political entertainment.

One feels that this danger would soon pass, and that Parliament and democracy would be enormously strengthened if Westminster opened its doors to television and radio without qualification or inhibition, and without any attempt at imposing a censorship on how reporting is to be done. As Aneurin Bevan, one of the greatest of Parliamentarians, declared: 'In these days when all the apparatus of mass suggestion are against democratic education we should seriously consider re-establishing intelligent communication between the House of Commons and the electorate as a whole. That, surely, is a democratic processs' On the same theme, Robin Day recently argued that TV would help bring Parliament closer to the young generation instead of appearing remote: 'If Parliament is getting weaker as the Executive grows stronger, television would help to strengthen the influence of Parliament against the despotism of the state'. In time, 'live' and unedited programmes of Parliamentary events will, one hopes, become just as important and accepted in national affairs as the live broadcasts of Wembley cup finals and internationals have become in sport.

APPENDIX

abc of Parliamentary terms

For the layman who wants to understand Parliament in broad outline without being overwhelmed by too much detail, here is a survey and explanation of some of the main features and terms of the Westminster scene which may add to an increased appreciation of the working of Parliament.

AFFIRMATION AND OATH–An MP cannot take his seat without first taking the Oath of Allegiance and signing the roll, but if, either for religious or non-religious reasons, he has conscientious objections to swearing on the Bible, he has the option to make a solemn declaration or affirmation that he will be faithful and bear true allegiance to the Queen. The oath reads: 'I swear by Almighty God that I will be faithful and bear true allegiance to Her Majesty Queen Elizabeth, her heirs and successors, according to law, so help me God'. The affirmation, usually by atheists or agnostics, says: 'I solemnly, sincerely and truly declare and affirm that I will be faithful and bear true allegiance to Her Majesty Queen Elizabeth, her heirs and successors, according to law'.

BACKBENCH MPS – These are the rank-and-file MPs who do not hold office of any kind in Government or in the Opposition 'Shadow' Cabinet, and accordingly do not share in the privilege of sitting on either of the two front benches. They occupy, instead, the back benches, where at least they enjoy greater freedom even if they do not share the responsibility of power.

BAR OF THE HOUSE – This is a line of demarcation, in this case a broad strip of leather, which marks off the official Chamber reserved for MPs only. When someone has committed a grave contempt or breach of privilege he is summoned to the 'Bar of the House' where he is reprimanded, rebuked or censured by Mr. Speaker – a solemn event which may also be invoked against an MP who is found guilty of breaking the rules of conduct.

BLUE BOOKS AND WHITE PAPERS – The distinction is that Blue Books are mostly official reports from Royal Commissions and special inquiries which are bulky and are published in blue paper covers at commercial book rates by the Stationery Office; while White Papers are mostly statements of Government and departmental policies and are very much briefer (identified in official jargon as 'Command Papers').

BREACH OF PRIVILEGE – If someone is accused and convicted of this offence, leading to the summons demanding his presence at the Bar of the House, it is because he has offended against and breached and insulted the dignity of Parliament. These are the most common breaches of the privilege of Parliament:

Assault, threat or abuse of an MP on account of his conduct as Member;
Defamation of the House or a Member because of his conduct or record;
Disorderly conduct at the House;

Attempts to bribe or threaten an MP in order to influence his conduct.

This survey only touches the fringe of PRIVILEGE: many large books, like Erskine May's authoritative work, have been written on the subject to guide the experts, but nowadays privilege is not the awesome subject it used to be in the early days when it was essential to establish the Privileges of Parliament as the first defence of democracy.

The chief privileges enjoyed by MPS are freedom of speech and freedom of arrest. So that Members may feel uninhibited in speaking the truth as they see it no action for defamation may be taken against them arising out of what they have said in the Commons or in official Committees, or what they have written in any Question or Motion tabled in the House (which thereby excludes slander and libel actions). This does not mean of course that Members have complete licence to say what they like because the House may be trusted to check any abuse of its privileges. Freedom from arrest, especially within the precincts of the Palace of Westminster, is more a formality nowadays, because MPS do not enjoy exemption from arrest or imprisonment for indictable offences within the criminal code. There are a great many other privileges, but they are seldom invoked; Parliamentary privilege is part of the country's legal system, appropriate to the phrase of the 'High Court of Parliament', including the power to send people to prison for contempt or breach of privilege – as well as the right to expel an MP whom the House decides is no longer fit to remain a Member because of some serious misconduct or conviction for grave misdemeanours.

BUDGET – This is the Chancellor of the Exchequer's fiscal and economic proposals for financing the country and running its economy, which he announces in his annual speech or statement known as his Budget. The name actually derives from a French term meaning a leather bag, like a brief case containing documents. Changes in taxation announced by the Chancellor in his Budget are subsequently enacted in the Finance Bill, the effective vehicle for fiscal policies.

SELECT COMMITTEES are appointed and empowered to conduct special inquiries into, for example, departmental estimates and public spending – the latest is a powerful Select Committee on expenditure – and to report direct to the House. The Select Committee procedure is high-powered because it can compel the appearance of witnesses and documents; it is also the most successful in getting at the facts of any situation or problem.

SPECIALIST SELECT COMMITTEES represent the latest developments in modernizing Parliament. It has been the habit in recent years, in order to give power and freedom to all-party Committees, to probe policy and administration of specialized subjects through these committees: there have been Specialist Committees in recent years dealing exclusively with Science and Technology, Agriculture, Race Relations and Immigration, Education and Science. These Committees have proved enormously successful in focusing attention on special problems and revealing the facts. Their expansion would greatly enhance the authority of Parliament in dealing independently with sectors of Government policy which might otherwise remain neglected; but against this, critics argue that Specialist Committees, admittedly based on the American Congressional Committees, detract from and outflank the authority of the chamber of the House of Commons as the supreme forum.

STANDING COMMITTEES deal with the committee stage of Bills after they have received their Second Reading, comprising up to fifty MPs (depending on the importance of the Bills) and nominated according to the relative strengths of the Government and Opposition.

HANSARD – The official verbatim report of the proceedings and speeches, the colloquial term for which dates back to Thomas Hansard who started publishing the official record of debate in 1812. There has been no Hansard connected with the official daily reports since 1889, but the verbatim publication still retains the old family identity.

ORDERS OF THE DAY – Every afternoon, immediately after question hour, you will hear the Police echoing the call throughout the Palace of Westminster 'Orders of the Day' which is the announcement from the Speaker that the business set down in the Order Papers for that day is about to start: in short, that the priority of business set down in Parliament's own agenda for that day's sitting is now ready for consideration and debate.

PAIRS AND PAIRING – In important debates and divisions you may be puzzled by reading about so many MPs being 'paired'. It is the expedient for balancing absent Members. If an MP from the Government side wishes to be absent from the House for a variety of special reasons and thereby unable to vote for the Government in the division lobby at the end of the debate he arranges with an opposition MP similarly placed to pair with him: the effect of this compact is that both agree not to vote. In practice, pairing means that absentees from divisions are scored off against each other; it is an unofficial procedure operated by the whips of all parties, but not officially recognized by the House, to keep a firm control and check upon their party MPs, because under the Whipping system Members are not supposed to be absent, especially from important votes, unless 'paired' – thus making sure that the other side is also minus an equal number of Members when the division is called. Pairing in short is a self-balancing exercise in mutual insurance.

PROROGATION – The Queen prorogues Parliament at the end of each session until the new session opens, usually up to a week or so later.

'I SPY STRANGERS' – The House goes into secret session when this motion is moved by any Member and is accepted, without debate. Secret sessions, with few exceptions, are held only in wartime. In the last war Parliament sat in secret to enable Sir Winston Churchill to make important reports containing facts and figures which if disclosed in public, would have been of great value to the enemy and thus endangered the country's security. When the motion 'I Spy Strangers' is moved it is put to the House by the Speaker, and if approved, all strangers and newspapermen have to withdraw. It constitutes contempt for any MP to repeat anything said in secret session or for any report to be published about what took place.

SERJEANT AT ARMS AND BLACK ROD – The Serjeant at Arms is in charge of all the permanent Commons staff on behalf of the Speaker and controls all disciplinary powers in order to preserve order throughout the Commons end of the building. His powers apply to visitors in the public galleries and elsewhere who may cause disturbances and disorders – in such cases he can order the arrest of offenders, in most instances they remain in his care until the end of the sitting – and also to assist MPs who have been commanded to withdraw from the Chamber by Mr. Speaker. The Serjeant, in short, is the executive head for the internal administration of that sector of Westminster occupied by the Commons. He is in attendance in court-dress on the Speaker at all ceremonies and processions, bearing the Mace which is the symbol of the authority vested in him by the Queen.

His equivalent in the House of Lords is the Yeoman Usher of the Black Rod – the title refers to the black ebony wand with a golden lion at the top which is his staff of office. When Black Rod, among his many duties, is sent to summon 'the faithful Commons' to attend in the House of Lords to hear, for example, the Royal Assent given to Bills, the door of the Commons chamber is slammed ceremoniously in his face; he is not admitted until he states his business. This seemingly high-handed treatment is a reminder of earlier days when the Commons had to be constantly on guard against eavesdropping or interruption by the Kings or their courtiers.

BIBLIOGRAPHY

The Power of Parliament by Ronald Butt, Constable
Our Parliament by Strathearn Gordon, Cassell for Hansard Society
Parliament by W. Ivor Jennings, Cambridge University Press
The House of Commons at Work by Eric Taylor, Pelican
The Cabinet by Patrick Gordon Walker, Cape
The British Cabinet by John P. Mackintosh, Stevens and Sons
The British Constitution by W. Ivor Jennings, Cambridge University Press
The English Constitution by Walter Bagehot. Introduction by R. H. S. Crossman, C. A. Watts and Co.
Parliament from the Press Gallery by T. F. Lindsay, Macmillan
The Purpose of Parliament by Quintin Hogg, Blandford Press
British Political Parties by Robert McKenzie, Mercury Books
Our House by Alfred C. Bossom, People's Universities Press
A Parliamentary Dictionary by L. A. Abraham and S. C. Hawtrey, Butterworth
The Commons in Transition, The Study of Parliament Group, Edited by A. H. Hanson and Bernard Crick, Fontana
Encyclopaedia of Parliament, Wilding and Laundy, Cassell